GOD LOVES YOU
— *as much as* —
YOU LOVE YOUR
DOG

*For Jo –
You are so loved!
♡ Leslie V.*

GOD LOVES YOU
as much as
YOU LOVE YOUR DOG

LESLIE VICARY

PURSE-DOG PRESS

Unless otherwise indicated, all Scripture quotations are taken from the Holy Bible, New Living Translation, copyright © 1996, 2004, 2015 by Tyndale House Foundation. Used by permission of Tyndale House Publishers, a Division of Tyndale House Ministries, Carol Stream, Illinois 60188. All rights reserved.

Scripture quotations marked (NIV) are taken from the Holy Bible, New International Version®, NIV®. Copyright © 1973, 1978, 1984, 2011 by Biblica, Inc.™ Used by permission of Zondervan. All rights reserved worldwide.

Scripture quotations marked (ESV) are from The ESV® Bible (The Holy Bible, English Standard Version®), copyright © 2001 by Crossway, a publishing ministry of Good News Publishers. Used by permission. All rights reserved.

Scripture quotations marked (GNT) are from the Good News Translation in Today's English Version-Second Edition Copyright © 1992 by American Bible Society. Used by Permission.

Scripture quotations marked (BSB) are from The Holy Bible, Berean Study Bible, BSB Copyright ©2016, 2020 by Bible Hub, Used by Permission. All Rights Reserved Worldwide.

Scripture quotations marked (AMP) are taken from the Amplified® Bible, (copyright © 2015 by The Lockman Foundation. Used by permission. www.lockman.org

Copyright © 2022 by Leslie Vicary. All rights reserved.

Printed in the United States of America.

No portion of this book may be reproduced or used in any form or by any electronic or mechanical means, including information storage and retrieval systems, without prior written permission of the copyright owner, except for the use of brief quotations for book reviews.

This book is not intended as a substitute for medical advice. The resources in this book are provided for informational purposes only and should not be used to replace the specialized training and professional judgment of a health care or mental health care professional.

The events in this book are memories from the author's perspective. Some anecdotes are included with the permission of the persons involved. Other illustrations are composites of real situations and any resemblance to people living or dead is coincidental. The author has not been compensated for brand mentions in any way.

For inquiries about discounted bulk orders or personal appearances please e-mail hello@pup-epiphanies.com.

Edited by: Nancy Lohr and Tom Siebert
Cover art by: Psyche
Photograph of the author by: Jessica with A Wall of Memories, LLC
Interior Design by: KUHN Design Group | kuhndesigngroup.com

ISBN Paperback: 979-8-9871995-2-7
ISBN Ebook: 979-8-9871995-0-3

PURSE-DOG
PRESS

DOWNLOAD YOUR FREE BONUS CHAPTER!

Thank you for purchasing

God Loves You as Much as You Love Your Dog.

To say thank you, I'd like to give you a bonus chapter from the next book in the Pup-epiphanies series for **FREE**.

go to

pages.pup-epiphanies.com/chapter

And if you haven't purchased this book yet, it's okay.

Consider this link an invitation to try out the Pup-epiphanies series on me.

l-r Leslie, Sugarbell, Eden, Sunflower, Jeff, Sailor

For Jeff
*my cohort in all things puppy
and otherwise,*

and for Eden
*the sweetest, prettiest girl
in the whole wide world.*

and for Sailor.

Contents

Introduction 11

Significant Need for a Swiffer 15

Dumber and Sweeter 25

God's Gift to Traffic 35

Sailor Napoleon Catfish Johnson 43

Unleashed 51

Bark and Keep On Barking 59

A Crevasse Named Desire 67

A Miserable Mess 77

I'm Not Here 85

Yard Full of Lard 93

Whiny Little Man Dog 101

Hornets to Hyenas 109

The Judgement 117

Made New 125

Q & A 135

Acknowledgements 143

Author Bio 147

Introduction

In a recent workshop, I was asked to close my eyes and think of the friend from my childhood with whom I felt completely at home and trusted without reservation. The first friend that sprang to mind was Lady, our family's golden retriever. That's right, a dog. Bringer of sticks, shaker of hands, protector, and my most trusted friend. No one could keep a secret like Lady.

We love our dogs, don't we? But why? They have no way of taking care of themselves. They need constant attention, correction, provision, and affection. And let's not even talk about the house-breaking phase when they need someone to open the door every three hours all night long. The only thing dogs require that they're actually capable of returning is love. And, weirdly, that's enough. No matter how high maintenance they may be, we adore these funny, mischievous, needy, sweet things.

Once Jesus was asked which commandment was the greatest. He answered "You must love the Lord your God with all your heart, all your soul, and all your mind" (Matthew 22:37). There are a lot of commandments. I would have guessed the most important ones were all the things we shouldn't do, like murdering somebody or running around on your husband. But no, Jesus said the most important thing is to love Him. Well, I'm thrilled to hear that, because it's about the only thing I'm capable of returning to Him in exchange for all the provision, protection, affection, and attention He constantly gives me. And, weirdly, that's enough for Him. *I* am the funny, mischievous, needy, sweet thing God adores.

So much of my relationship with my dogs reminds me of God's relationship with me. Interestingly, each of my dogs illustrates a specific spiritual topic. Sugarbell struggles with fear and anxiety, Sunflower exudes joy, etc. Navigating their individual charms and challenges has helped shape my view of God and of myself, so I'm devoting a book to each of my furry children.

In order of birth, our dogs are: Tampa, a lab of immense stature and, uh, enthusiasm; Sailor, my sweet bichon; Sugarbell, my daughter's spitfire Maltese mix; Sunflower, our exuberant shih tzu mix; and Clover, the bichon baby with all that being the baby encompasses.

God's character is clearly revealed to me through my experiences with our dogs. Succinctly put by my friend Kelli: "Puppies are your love language." And she's right. God speaks to me through my animals (not literally, thank goodness, because that would be unsettling). God knows us each so well and talks to us in a way that resonates with us personally. If you don't think that God speaks to you, you probably just haven't heard Him in your language yet. But you can. As Eli advised Samuel, "Say 'Speak Lord, your servant is listening'" (1 Samuel 3:9).

This book is the true story of Sailor, a little dog whom I deeply loved, and how my love for him helped me understand how much God loves me. I hope it reminds you of how very dear you are to the God who adores you.

*The L̴ord is merciful and compassionate,
slow to get angry and filled with unfailing love.
The Lord is good to everyone.
He showers compassion on all his creation.*

PSALM 145:8–9

Significant Need for a Swiffer

*Hope deferred makes the heart sick,
but a dream fulfilled is a tree of life.*

PROVERBS 13:12

When I was single, I wanted a fluffy little dog more than anything. Of course, I also wanted better boyfriends, fewer fat cells, and world travel, but a puppy seemed like the more achievable goal at the time. I would see people prancing their prissy, toy dogs around the park near my apartment and wanted one so badly! I imagined breezing around town with a diminutive fluff ball in the passenger seat of my Miata. She would covertly accompany me to music festivals stashed in my oversized bag. She'd enjoy pet-sized mock lattes at my favorite outdoor cafe. Passersby wouldn't be able to resist stopping to admire my fun-size canine.

But who was I kidding? This was a poorly considered pipe dream. I didn't have time for a dog. I was rarely home. I didn't have a yard. A bored, lonely dog would do nothing but eat the furniture and bark all day. A dog was out of the question. But I swore to myself that someday I, too, would have a fluffy little buddy who would go everywhere with me, preferably in my purse.

Fast forward. Jeff Vicary and I met. Online! Jeff Vicary and I got married. In person! We also planned to be married people in person, so I quit my job, sold my convertible, closed my bank account, and ditched Birmingham, Alabama, to move to a small village[1] in Illinois. My mind boggles at the choices I made. Go big or go home. Except I couldn't go home, because I had sold my car and quit my job.

Suddenly life was weirdly domestic, overflowing to a surreal degree with things like family potlucks and leaf blowing. Where just months prior I had been an independent woman with her own office and a social calendar, now my husband went to work and I was at home, alone, all day. All. Day. To say the least, I was experiencing culture shock and extreme boredom. But on the upside, I had a house, a yard, and a whole lot of time. My life was finally puppy-ready.

With all this newfound leisure on my hands, I was free to spend what used to be workdays sitting at the kitchen table, internet shopping for dogs. I forwarded so many photos to my lucky new husband. "Hey, honey, how's work? Here's a pic of some puppies taking a bubble bath wearing party hats. Can you even stand it? Have a good day!" I had a lot of time and energy to channel. And he survived it.

Jeff, who in his life had only owned one dog, a spaniel remembered mainly for its incessant barking prior to the inevitable re-homing, was unconvinced that we needed a dog. Despite the obvious appeal of the photos I forwarded, he did not exhibit an appropriate level of enthusiasm. In response to my photos of delicate toy poodles in tiaras, he would send back a photo of chubby, little, roly-poly

---

1. I could never get used to calling it a "village" as is common in the Midwest. Every time I said it, I felt the impulse to put on a bonnet and call somebody "Pa." All villages shall heretofore be referred to as towns.

retrievers romping through leaves. As I would soon discover, it wasn't that he didn't want a dog; he didn't want a small dog.

Every night we searched through the so-you-want-a-puppy websites, which I highly recommend. These sites offer matchmaking quizzes with insightful questions such as: How many days a week would you enjoy exercising outdoors with your pet?" or "How many dollars a month would you like to spend on grooming?" Mystifyingly, none of them ever asked "How many hours a day would you like to spend vacuuming up dog hair from your hardwoods?", which is a grievous omission if they're going to lead someone to select a large, shedding dog, such as, say, a Labrador retriever.

Ask me how many hours a day Jeff Vicary enjoyed taking these quizzes. I'll tell you. Many. It became his obsession. Much to my dismay, all of his searches returned large, high-energy dogs like retrievers, spaniels, and coon hounds. Growing up southern, I'd had one of all of these breeds including a hound of questionable heritage named Oscar, who nightly sat on top of the dog house and howled until one night someone, who shall remain nameless (my dad), fired a shot over his head to shut him up. (Did I mention we were in the South?)[2]

I knew Jeff and I were never in a million years getting any of these big dogs, but I humored my new husband and listened as he enthusiastically read me the extensive lists of dog attributes that, oddly enough, did not include anything about prolific shedding or nightly howling. Again, grievous omissions.

I didn't care what some website said. I had spent years living all the scenarios of small dog ownership in my mind. We were getting a toy poodle. Jeff and I married in June, and I spent the next six weeks priming my husband to welcome the previously described tiny ball of fluff to our family.

---

[2]. I'm not endorsing anyone's actions, just telling the story like I remember it.

Cut to August.

When I returned from visiting my parents for a few days, Jeff met me in the driveway. "Surprise! Meet your new dog!" he exclaimed and gestured to an unbelievably cute, although completely unwanted, twelve-pound, seven-week-old yellow lab. This puppy wouldn't fit in my purse currently, much less in another year. My eyes dropped to her feet, the best forecaster of future dog size, and, honest to goodness, this puppy had feet the size of a full-grown dog. It would be like a toddler wearing a size seven women's shoe. This was not going to be some sixty-five-pound lab in adulthood. This was a heifer.

Jeff was so thrilled with his surprise that I quelled my instinct to throw my suitcase at him. It wouldn't have done any good anyhow. He already adored her, and she adored him. It was all very much man and man's best friend/girlfriend. As I later learned, while I was out of town, he had gone to a farm, chosen her from the litter, then spent three days bonding with her before presenting my "gift." He really thought he had created this romantic, dream-fulfilling, cinematic scenario, but you can imagine my bitter disappointment. Marriage is a study in growth and forgiveness. And you both get a chance to be the one who grows and the one who forgives. As it was, their relationship was sealed, and I was shnookered. He had his lab, and I had a new and substantial need for a Swiffer sweeper.

The next morning, Jeff left for work, and suddenly Tampa was my responsibility, much to both of our distress. I was at a loss as to how to manage that dog. To this day I have little white scars on my forearms from the many times she mercilessly gnawed on them. Copious hours were spent on my new pastimes: dissuading her from rolling on top of and then eating the spectacular bed of flowers I was cultivating, vacuuming up unfathomable quantities of dog hair (as mentioned), and chasing her across the yard in failed attempts to save the birds she yanked right out of the birdbath. It is not an exaggeration to say she was the worst puppy in the world. As expressed by Jeff's seven-year-old niece who had come over to play with her: "I didn't know she would be this bad. I'm ready to go home."

Even after she was grown, Tampa was all puppy, all 110 pounds of her. Eventually, through shared trauma if nothing else, Tampa and I became friends. I'll never forget teaching her to "talk" to me while I repainted the kitchen. She sounded just like Chewbacca from Star Wars, and I thought of myself as Han Solo, holding entire conversations with a Wookie as we navigated this weird new suburban world. To be honest, Tampa was a great source of companionship. But just because I'd come to appreciate her oversized charms didn't mean I was giving up on getting my purse-dog. This was just a detour.

Oh, life. Such a zigzag. Why can't it be linear? Move from point A to B, with no interruptions, no detours, like a dad on a mission to get from Green Bay to Orlando in a single day. But do you know what that trip is? It's boring. Personally I like a trip that includes a

The feet, y'all. The feet.

couple of peach-stand stops or something. Funny how I prefer the scenic route on a trip, but not so much in life. Setbacks, miscalculations, reroutes, compromise. They're an undesirable, if not predictable, part of the trek towards any goal.

My disappointment with Tampa was in no way as dramatic or consequential as the story I'm about to reference, but stay with me.

In Genesis, the story of Joseph is a striking illustration of how God can work things out in our favor, no matter how disappointing the circumstance. Our hero, Joseph, experiences a series of shocking betrayals, starting with his own brothers selling him into slavery, followed closely by false accusations of rape, then years of unjust imprisonment. Major detours. It must have been challenging to trust God through all of these injustices, but he did. Then, in a long-awaited twist, God moves Joseph out of prison and into a position of great authority and influence in the Egyptian government, one of the most powerful governments in the world at the time.

Eventually, Joseph's brothers—the ones who sold him into slavery— were forced to come crawling to him for food to survive a famine. At first, they didn't recognize him, but when they did, it was (understandably) much to their terror. Is this not the perfect revenge fantasy? Think of all the ways he could have gotten them back. Amazingly, Joseph took the high road and didn't gloat or take revenge. His response to their apologies was "No worries" (paraphrase mine). "You intended to harm me, but God intended it all for good" (Genesis 50:20). Then he took his brothers in, met all of their needs, and didn't even rub his fabulous new life in their faces. Talk about someone who had managed to find the benefit in hurtful happenings and move on! It's a saga. You can read the whole sordid story in Genesis, chapter 37 and chapters 39 through 45.

Joseph's patient trust that God would work everything out in his favor was not misplaced. God did miraculously turn things around.

And He does the same today. Disappointing detours can sprout into His best blessings.

My situation with Tampa was disappointing for sure, but it was not over. It was just sprouting. And seeds take time. Like Joseph, I had to trust that, no matter how it felt, God would work things out in my favor.

*Let us not become weary in doing good,
for at the proper time we will reap
a harvest if we do not give up.*

GALATIANS 6:9 NIV

The Point

God can work things out in your favor,
no matter how disappointing the circumstance.

Journal Prompts

- What is an expected detour you have experienced?
- What did you learn from the experience?
- How have you seen God work a disappointing situation to your benefit?
- How does this impact your view of future delays and disappointments?

Let's Pray

Lord, You are El Shaddai, the Lord God Almighty. You are greater than I can even imagine. Thank You that even in Your vastness, You care about the small details of my life. Please forgive me for the times I worry instead of trusting You. Please help me to have patience, believing that You will turn detours into benefits.

To Play

"Steady Me" by Hollyn featuring Aaron Cole[3]

---

3. There's a suggested song for every chapter. To listen, search the title and artist. The first result is usually a link to the song on the artist's Youtube channel. Or you can listen to all the songs in this book with my free playlist at pages.pup-epiphanies.com/playlist

Dumber and Sweeter

God decided in advance to adopt us into his own family by bringing us to himself through Jesus Christ. This is what he wanted to do, and it gave him great pleasure.

EPHESIANS 1:5

Our veterinarian skewed more toward Dr. Doolittle than medical professional. His practice was beautiful chaos. A cat blocked the pens as she lounged on the check-in shelf, a parrot noisily dangled above the receptionist's file cabinets, and a canine patiently overcame his cone of shame to awkwardly sniff my ankles. It was like that all the time.

As the vet performed Tampa's routine exam, I informed him that I had not given up on my dream of having a small dog and asked his opinion on dog breeds, though this was really just a courtesy. He was being deftly maneuvered down a path whose inevitable end would be agreement that a miniature poodle was the ideal candidate. However, not one to be easily manipulated, he veered off the intended path into a list of undesirable poodle traits.

1. They often attach to a single person and merely tolerate (if you're lucky) the rest of the family.

2. They can be vindictive if you displease them, retaliating with behavior such as pooping in your shoes.

3. They eventually exert dominance over the entire household, ruling you instead of you ruling them.

He summarized with this highly quotable advice: "Poodles are too smart. Get a bichon. They're dumber and sweeter."[4]

The search for a bichon breeder was on. I quickly settled on one in Iowa, a farmer. An Iowa farmer. Is that not just the most flag-waving-toddler-at-a-small-town-parade thing you've ever heard? He lived up to friendly Midwesterner expectations and sent me a video of his little girl playing out back in the barn, holding up the puppy that would eventually be my puppy. He forwarded photos of past litters in their idyllic new lives, perching on the bows of boats or stuffed into Christmas stockings. I was so sold. And for what seemed like an astronomical amount at the time—$400—I clicked "submit" and had a due date on the calendar. You cannot overestimate my enthusiasm for this event.[5]

After what seemed like months—not weeks—of waiting, the drop-off day finally arrived. One chilly morning in October, thick with fog over the barren Illinois cornfields, I drove in the predawn silence to

---

4. Apologies to the poodles. And also to the bichons.
5. Years later, when we were thinking of getting another bichon, I would attempt to find this Iowa farmer, but the only search result was a grainy night-vision video of a puppy mill raid on this Iowa farmer's "barn." Sailor was the product of a puppy mill? But I thought puppy mill dogs had health problems, physical defects, and personality defects. Sailor was a beautiful, happy, mostly healthy dog. In actuality, puppy mills may produce perfectly robust puppies, but the parent dogs are living confined, often filthy, overbred lives. They are treated as a commodity, not a pet, which is heartbreaking. I now recommend making a home visit to your breeder or adopting a sweet shelter dog.

Dumber and Sweeter

Baby Sailor with bells on.

pick up my new baby. Prickly with anticipation, I pulled into the designated meeting place for my Iowan drop-off. I felt like a spy, backed into a parking spot, watching the front door of the hotel, fog so dense all you could see were auras of light radiating from the street lamps. Eventually, a massive figure emerged from the mist, a man in classic farmer overalls, with scruffy facial hair and work boots, cradling a bit of white fluff in his enormous hands. He dropped this delicate creature into my regular-sized hands, and the puppy of my dreams was really, truly, *finally* mine!

What happened next is inexplicable. I opened the SUV tailgate and placed this frightened baby animal in a cold, lonely crate. At least I had filled it with blankets, a ticking clock, and the things they recommend to make your puppy feel safe and comfortable. I clearly had read the well-meaning advice of animal experts and followed it against all common sense. Why don't they recommend putting him in your coat, close to your warm ticking heart? Sure, sure. A crate in the back is the safest place. I get it. But tell it to the puppy piteously crying all the way home.

When I finally got my frightened friend back to the house and had a good look at him (and a whiff of him), I realized this little guy smelled like a kennel of coyotes, and his nails were sloth-level long. My mind screamed back to a page in my *Guinness Book of World Records* that I bought at the sixth-grade book fair. A man, whose nails had never been trimmed, held up his hands, exhibiting fingernails that curled in foot-long spirals from his fingertips. My twelve-year-old self would lie in bed at night and think of this photo. So many questions. How does he open doors? Can he drive a car? How does he wash his hair? Can he make a sandwich? If he breaks a nail, will he just cut them all off or glue the broken one back on? It boggled the sixth-grade mind. And the disgusting state of the new fur-baby boggled my current mind.

The original plan had been to immediately take the new puppy to meet Jeff, the same husband who did not want a small dog. There was no way I was showing up with this hot mess for a first impression. So the puppy spa experience commenced, starting with a shampoo in the bathroom sink. His soggy appearance gave the phrase "drowned rat" deep personal significance. He was breathtaking. Not in the good way.

And here's a testament to how fortunate it was that I didn't come home with an actual human baby: after I washed and dried him, I went to another room for something and left him unattended on the bathroom counter. Fortunately I also left the cosmetics drawer open; so instead of falling three feet to the ground, he fell three inches into an assortment of eyeshadows. Whew. This dog. His day just kept getting better. I'd had him for an hour, and so far he'd been locked in a crate, dropped in a drawer, and bathed; and we hadn't even been to the vet for the nail clipping yet. (Somebody had to do it, and that somebody was definitely not me.)

When we were finally done with the traumatizing grooming portion of our day, my new best friend was back in the car, riding up front with me, despite all expert advice. He was no longer crying in a crate but cozied down in a crossbody handbag made into a snug little bed where he sleepily (and perhaps suspiciously) watched me from the passenger seat. I could hardly take my eyes off of the unbearable cuteness that was soon to be named Sailor, not even to drive.

When we arrived at the office, Jeff looked at me with confusion and asked where the dog was. I gestured toward the cottony head peeking above the opening of my bag. His reaction was like Christmas

First meeting. Pre-chaos.

morning in a house of toddlers: surprise, wonder, joy, maybe some unnatural squealing. He kept saying that he couldn't believe a dog could be so small and proudly carried our puppy around the office, showing him off to coworkers, as if Sailor was his biological offspring or something. The man who did not want a small dog was smitten. Ah, victory!

Sailor represented so much more than a new puppy to me. I didn't quite realize the magnitude of the sacrifices I had made when I moved to Illinois. I had quit the job I loved, sold the convertible I also loved, traded downtown for the suburbs, and exchanged sidewalk cafes with friends for family potlucks. In my grief for the life I lost, Sailor was the huggable proof that God had not forgotten about me way up there in the cold Midwest. My sorrow was not trivial to Him. What mattered to me mattered to God. In Isaiah 61 He promises to replace grief with joy. And he did!

If American Gothic had been a painting about dogs at Christmas.

When Sailor first came to us, his whole self was exactly half the size of Tampa's head. He was so tiny and his footsteps so silent that we had to tie bells around his neck to avoid accidentally stepping on him. This in no way meant that he was limited by his diminutive stature. Quite the opposite. He wielded it like a weapon. Almost from arrival, he was the boss, ceaselessly antagonizing Tampa, much to our amusement. His favorite game was to sprint across the house, pounce on Tampa's head, tug on her ears, then tear back across the house in a game of "can't catch me," only to avoid her retribution by cleverly hiding underneath Tampa's belly where she couldn't reach him.

Having two puppies in the house was utter, wonderful mayhem. Life was so much more fun and hilarious with two. Jeff had his big ole leaf jumper, and I finally had the precocious little fluff ball I had dreamed of for so long. Because of the Tampa detour, the new puppy experience was made exponentially better. God took a disappointment and made it one of my best blessings. I had never even considered having two puppies! True to his word, I got more than I had hoped for or imagined (see Ephesians 3:20–21)![6]

And we know that for those who love God all things work together for good.

ROMANS 8:28 ESV

---

6. For more photos and videos of the dogs visit instagram.com/leslievicary/

The Point

What matters to you matters to God.

Journal Prompts

- Have you ever felt grief for a part of your life that passed?
- How did you feel God's presence in those moments?
- How do you see God replacing grief with joy?
- When have you felt like God answered prayer with even more than you had asked for?

Let's Pray

You are Jehovah Shamma, the God who is with me, even in sorrow and grief. Thank You for promising to restore and bring good out of everything. Forgive me for the times I doubt Your goodness. Please help me to see all the ways You give me even more than I have hoped for.

To Play

"The Goodness" by Toby Mac and Blessing Offor

God's Gift to Traffic

*I pray that God, the source of hope,
will fill you completely with joy and
peace because you trust in him.*

ROMANS 15:13

Joy. Sailor spread it. Just taking him in the car with me was a service to humanity. As soon as Sailor stuck his happy head out into the breeze, entire traffic jams transformed. Passenger-seated people would point him out to their drivers. Children roused from their devices to giggle at something actual. They rolled down their windows and screamed their questions at me. "What's his name?"

"Sailor."

"Does he eat?" (kids)

"Uh-huh."

"What do you feed him?"

"Banana popsicles and broccoli."[7]

People on all sides of our vehicle found themselves experiencing delight, despite the fact that they were on the fourth cycle of the light.

---

7. "Dog food" is such a predictable answer. Why not give them something to think about?

Sailor's gladness to be in the middle of the world somewhere, even in a clump of unmoving cars, rubbed off on people. "A cheerful look brings joy to the heart" (Proverbs 15:30). Even in traffic.

Not only was he the darling of the morning commute, but Sailor was also the joy of the bike trail. There is a greenway that we often would bike, me driving, him in the dog carrier in the back.[8] Everyone who passed would comment, usually about his chill demeanor, with an arm flung casually over the back of his padded carrier and head lolled back, watching the leaves go by overhead. Contrast our dog, Sunflower, who is an exuberant, frenetic, hazard on the back of a bike, constantly moving from side to side, debating which of my hips hides the better view. She throws the balance so far off we've nearly wobbled into the river many times. But not Sailor. He was so chill he was practically meditative, the Matthew McConaughey of the Swamp Rabbit Trail.[9]

And he was completely game. The rest of my family has not always (read *almost never*) been enthusiastic to go on bike rides with me, so much so that I've requested a family bike outing for Mother's Day many times. It's the one day I can coerce them to do whatever I want without complaint. But I never had to convince Sailor. He was good to go anywhere I wanted anytime. And he made the whole experience so joyful. To glance back and see him slung out, tongue out, smiling back at me was just joy. And not just to me. He lit up every path we traveled.

Joy is contagious. I think that's part of why people love having animals around. Animals never grow out of their enthusiasm for life. Everything is exciting. All I have to do is pick up my tennis shoes and the dogs skip around my feet, thrilled out of their minds to go for an adventure (read *walk around the block*). At the slightest provocation,

---

8. In case you were wondering.
9. This used to be a quiet, local greenway, but now Greenville is on all the best-places-to-visit lists and the whole world thinks they're Lance Armstrong. "ON YOUR LEFT!"

they're convinced something amazing is about to happen. What a gift to never dull to everyday pleasures.

Thinking of that zeal for adventure reminds me of the day Jeff and I moved into our home in Charleston.[10] I was walking Sailor and Tampa around the yard, keeping them out of the way while the movers were loading things into our new home. At some point, I lost my grip on Sailor's leash, and he took off, darting around trees and under shrubs to escape me. He was just a couple of months old and still really small and quick. I was definitely no match for his agility, and he got away from me. I panicked. We searched everywhere, but there was no sign of him. Then I wondered if he could have run into the house, since the doors were open. I raced from room to room, searching under beds and behind boxes, and found nothing. But then I opened the bathroom door, and there was little Sailor, cheerfully grinning at me, soaking wet, sitting in the toilet. IN the toilet. He splashed his paws into the bowl, gleefully barking at the flying toilet water, panting happily, yipping at me as if inviting me to play in the toilet too. It was like he was saying, "Look, Mom, this place has a pool!"

It was impossible to be mad at Sailor. Even when he was getting in trouble, he was still bringing the joy. He had the heart of an explorer or an escape artist, depending on who you're asking. If I opened the front door, he would attempt to dart out between my feet. When someone rang the bell, you could only crack the door to peek out with just one eye or Sailor was gone. One day I failed to block him, and he took his shot, running out the door and down the street. Of course, I was barefoot, chasing him through the neighborhood. He wasn't as hard to catch as you might guess, because he was pausing at literally every surface he could lift a leg on. He claimed all the mailboxes, several sweetgrass shrubs, a garbage bin, and someone's Toyota

---

10. Back where it's balmy, praise the Lord.

God's gift to traffic, right there.

before I caught up with him. Euphoric in his conquests, he didn't even resist when I swept him up. He just reveled. You gotta love that spunk.

Sailor brought so much joy to my life. Unintentionally. He brought joy because he experienced joy. He had an unbridled enthusiasm for life. And he was fearless. On our first trip to the beach with the dogs, he ran straight into the waves while our retriever (the water dog) cowered back. At the dog park, he would sidle his fluffy self up to the loudest, roughest pack of big dogs, expecting to play. And he was the muscle, standing protectively between timid Tampa and any hundred-pounder who dared to challenge him. Such a little stud.

Listen to this definition of joy. It speaks to exactly what I believe to be true about Sailor. Joy is "a feeling of extreme happiness or cheerfulness, especially related to the acquisition or expectation of something good."[11] That differs a little from the way joy is presented in the

---

11. Joy. 2022. In Wordhippo.com. Retrieved August 26, 2022 from https://www.wordhippo.com/what-is/the-meaning-of-the-word/joy.html

Bible. Biblically, joy is something that is experienced because of our relationship with God. It isn't reliant on circumstances but is *only* reliant on the presence of the Holy Spirit. When we know Jesus, we can be full of joy regardless of what is going on in our lives. We can have "cheerfulness related to the expectation of something good" because we trust in God's goodness and sovereignty over every situation.

Sailor had hopeful expectations in every situation, never dread or fear. Fear prevents joy. It's like the flu shot. Inject fear and you won't get joy, or if you do, it will be low-grade and won't last long. Have you ever tried to live with cheerful expectations while you're worried? It's not even possible. They're opposites!

Jesus is the antidote to fear. "There is no fear in love, but perfect love casts out fear" (1 John 4:18 ESV). Jesus is love. It's not something He does; it's who He is. His very essence casts out fear. Fear has no place in His presence. So the more we experience His presence, the less dominant fear and worry become in our lives. In the Bible joy is listed as one of the fruits produced by the Holy Spirit, meaning that when you've received Jesus as your Savior, you are given the supernatural ability to live with joy, despite circumstances. It's something that wells up as a byproduct of the Holy Spirit of God dwelling in you. When we have Jesus, we have the God-given power to live in cheerful expectation of something good, no matter what is happening around us (see Galatians 5:22–23).

*The LORD is my strength and my shield;
my heart trusts in him, and he helps me.
My heart leaps for joy, and with
my song I praise him.*

PSALM 28:7 NIV

The Point

In Jesus, we have the supernatural ability to be joyful in any circumstance.

Journal Prompts

- When was a time you felt a cheerful expectation of something good?
- When was a time you felt anxious or fearful?
- What role does your relationship with Jesus play in joy and in fear?
- How can you invite the presence of Jesus into your day?

Let's Pray

Lord, you are Jehovah-Nissi, the banner over us. Thank You that we can trust that You are always with us, fighting on our behalf, as in battle. Thank You for the hope and the miraculous victories that Your banner represents. Forgive me for complaining and worrying. Train me to expect something good and to trust You so I can live in joy, regardless of circumstances.

To Play

"Joyful" by Dante Bowe

Sailor Napoleon Catfish Johnson

"I have called you by name, you are mine."

ISAIAH 43:1 ESV

Despite my usual assertion that Sailor was the perfect canine companion, even I must admit that he had his flaws. One of his nicknames was Catfish, for a couple of reasons. First, when he came in from outside on a warm day, he smelled like either a catfish or a fifth grader after recess and "Fifth-grader-after-recess" is too long for a nickname. Second, he was a bottom feeder, eating anything that he might find on the ground. It was incredible to behold. I'm forever scarred by the images that popped up while researching how to get a dog to stop eating whatever he might find lying around the yard. I wish the experience on no one.

Another less than savory trait: Sailor was bossy. Honestly earning his other nickname of Napoleon, he suffered the classic small-man syndrome. Sailor, despite weighing only twelve pounds, lorded it over 110-pound Tampa. He would stretch out on her extra-large bed, attempting to reach his four paws to the corners so there was no room left for her at all as she sat nearby, quietly whimpering. She would cast a helpless look over her shoulder at me, oblivious to her own magnitude, while one swat from her would have sent him flying across the room. It's curious to witness someone with so much latent power regard herself as helpless. But I'll save that for another day.

Sailor's other nickname of "Johnson" just ended his full name nicely, no real meaning except that it is a quintessential American surname, and he *was* an all-American farm boy, after all.

Though he had no other nicknames, he did have more terrible traits to offer. The first two would have been enough, but, alas, there's more, including the characteristic most likely to get you throat punched: mouth noise. The amount he produced was uncanny. He could sit completely still, not doing anything but breathing, and yet make mouth noise. No amount of hydration extinguished the crinkly racket emanating from his mouth. For an indication of the cringe level this registered, ask someone to say "moist" three times slowly.

Even when the mouth noise mercifully paused, there was the licking. Sailor tirelessly tasted everything in reach: the tags on his collar, the sofa arm, the top of his right paw, the corner of his bed, the metal grid of the fireplace door. You name it. He was a licking machine. It wasn't even anxiety-induced. He just enjoyed it. As other dogs are to chew toys, Sailor was to household surfaces. A steady soundtrack of tongue friction against a multitude of textures played underneath our lives.

Unbearable as the licking may have been, it wasn't even his worst trait. The marking takes that trophy. Oh, man. We could never completely house train this dog. He destroyed my favorite crisp, white, oversized chair *and* its ottoman. He claimed them as his own by leaving large amber rings on every corner. Even professional cleaners couldn't return them to white. Over the years we replaced carpet, comforters, a mattress, cabinetry, and my favorite chair *and* ottoman—all because he refused to just pee on the bushes like a normal dog.

That is quite a list of offending behaviors for a dog whom I thought of as canine perfection. Understand, the only reason I direct attention to his less desirable attributes is to make this point: no matter how smelly, bossy, noisy, or destructive he could be, I adored Sailor. It brought me so much joy to walk into a room and be greeted by his cheerful little self.

By nature, bichons do not like to be away from their people, and Sailor definitely presented that trait. He was my canine shadow, following me from room to room, always near. He was my carline guy, officemate, bike trail buddy, and most excellent cleaner of floors during food prep.[12] His enthusiasm for my presence made me feel irreplaceable and special. I loved that his tail wagged at just the sound of my voice, and how he would rest his head on my arm and lick my hand to show his affection. Of course, he licked pretty much anything, as discussed, so I could be reading too much into that. Nevertheless, I loved him wholeheartedly.

Bike trail buddy.

It's incredible to me that God loves me, just as I loved Sailor, flaws and all. It blows my mind to think that as much as it pleased me to have Sailor near, it pleases God to have me near. My annoying habits do not deter him. People

---

12. Finally, his mastery of licking proved desirable.

can ditch out when things get messy, shocking us with the most unexpected acts of desertion and betrayal, often at just the time when we need them most. But not God. He has promised that "He will be with you; he will neither fail you nor abandon you" (Deuteronomy 31:8).

If your first instinct is to say "Yeah, right" when you hear that promise, then you must be basing your perception of God on your experience with people. No doubt, someone in your life has proven themselves to be imperfect (among other things), as people do. You need to know that their failure is not an indicator of God's trustworthiness. It's also not a statement about your worth.

When people betray you, there is a thought that will try to root in your mind: "I'm unlovable." This is a lie sent straight from hell to keep you from becoming the whole, joyful person God created you to be. Do not let that lie stay there, growing in your psyche. It will keep you from the abundant life you are promised. Let the truth of God's Word dig up that hideous weed. The truth is that you are loved and favored by the Most High God. His words to you are: "I have loved you with an everlasting love; I have drawn you with unfailing kindness" (Jeremiah 31:3 NIV). Everlasting. Unfailing.

God knows everything about you and loves you exactly as you are. You are unique, special, and irreplaceable to Him. The same God who created the magnificence of the cosmos created you. I mean, God, as in Yahweh, Creator of heaven and earth, the Great I Am. You are His design and He loves you. And He's not leaving. As undesirable as you can sometimes be (because we can all sometimes be), you are not a sad surprise to Him. God already knows your idiosyncrasies, and He loves you wholeheartedly.

Read that paragraph again.

If not for my experience with Sailor, it might be hard for me to believe that God still adores me, even when I'm a mess. But no matter how nerve-wracking or messy Sailor could be, I always wanted him near. I barely put him down. I'm holding him in practically every photo. Not once was I trying to put distance between us, even when he was at his worst. God feels the same way about you. He wants you near, no matter what. He adores you. Always. Even at your worst.

And if you're thinking you're too far gone, too weird, too messed up for God, read the Old Testament. You'll see God constantly coming up with ways He can cover the sins of His people so He can be in their presence. And these people were a mess. They were into all kinds of crazy stuff. Seriously. You have nothing on them. Their outrageous sins were a constant block to God's presence, but He consistently forgave them. Eventually God sent His own Son, Jesus, to cover all the sins of the whole world once and for all. Through Jesus, God removed every barrier that existed between us and Him because He loves us, flaws and all.

*The LORD is compassionate and merciful,
slow to get angry and filled with unfailing love.*
PSALM 103:8

The Point

God loves you just as you are, flaws and all.

Journal Prompts

- What role do you think your quirks play in your relationships with other people?
- Who is someone (person or pet) you have loved so much that their quirks didn't stop you from wanting to be around them?
- How does it feel to know that God always loves you, flaws and all?
- What does God's "unfailing love" and "unfailing kindness" mean to you?

Let's Pray

Lord, You are my shepherd, Jehovah Rohi, protectively leading and caring for me.[13] *Thank You for accepting me and loving me exactly as I am. Please forgive me for believing negative things about myself and sometimes seeing myself as unlovable, when You tell me very clearly that I am deeply loved by You. Help me to receive Your love and to love myself, flaws and all.*

To Play

"You Say" by Lauren Daigle

---

[13]. If you're curious about the names of God in the prayers in this book, download this free PDF to learn more about His names, what they mean and how they originated. pages.pup-epiphanies.com/names

Unleashed

*But you, Lord, are a shield around me,
my glory, the One who lifts my head high.*

PSALM 3:3 NIV

Sailor was eight when Sugarbell joined the family. She was a part Havanese, part Maltese, black-with-white-markings ball of frenzy brought by Santa. What was he thinking? This dog made Tampa seem sedate.

I'll never forget my six-year-old, still in her flannel Christmas gown, screaming through the halls, attempting to escape the tyranny of her new puppy. Three-pound Sugarbell spent Christmas Day ferociously herding everyone within charging distance. Our guests had to take a running leap to the sofa for refuge. If we needed to move about for any reason, we waited for her to be distracted and then raced to our destination.

Fortunately, Sugarbell's frenzy exhausted her. Almost in mid-sprint she would abruptly stop and pass out before she even hit the floor. It was a relief, however short-lived it may have been. Within minutes she would rise like a phoenix to terrorize her people anew. Amazingly, Eden's enthusiasm for Sugarbell was not deterred, and her love has never waned. Sugarbell's persnicketiness as a full-grown dog is surpassed only by her frenzy as a puppy.

Jeff and I had hoped that Sugarbell would not only be a much-loved friend for Eden but also a buddy for Sailor, since Tampa was no longer with us. Unfortunately, on Christmas Day, when Santa pranked us with Sugarbell, Sailor's only activity was doped up crate rest, having hurt his back. Any fantasy we had about Sailor and Sugarbell hitting it off was squashed by the day's furor. Sailor was in no way prepared to add her mayhem to his malaise.

Even after the injury healed, Sailor and the puppy were not a great match. Sugarbell was spritely and mischievous, constantly bouncing around him, begging for a game of chase. Sailor, despite his former puppy exuberance, had mellowed into a dog who was content to nap on a sunny patch of floor for most of the day. And like any old man, he didn't really want to be pounced on as he did so.

One afternoon, just after we had come in from a long walk, Sugarbell was still bursting with energy while Sailor seemed particularly exhausted by her antics. He slowly trudged toward the water bowl as his leash dragged the floor between his legs. Sugarbell dove for it, playfully growling and tugging him backward. When he attempted to ignore her and continue his trek, she gripped the leash more tightly in her teeth and yanked straight back. With every step he took forward, she pulled his neck lower and lower until his chin grazed the floor. He was helpless to escape her control.

Poor Sailor. He looked so tired, so sick of being harassed. Compassion for the little man moved me. I reached beneath his beleaguered chin and easily unhooked the leash from his collar, catapulting Sugarbell across the room. Sailor gratefully trotted over to me, sank to the floor with a groan, and fell asleep. His liberation was an easy win. For me.

Matthew 9:36 tells us that when Jesus saw the crowds, "He had compassion for them, because they were harassed and helpless, like sheep without a shepherd" (NIV). Can I tell you something? When you are helpless and harassed with somebody or something pulling you down, God notices. He is moved to compassion by your struggle. You may feel powerless to escape your situation, but what is impossible for you is an easy win for God.

When I think of Sailor struggling to even lift his head while under the control of Sugarbell, I think of destructive habits. They seem harmless enough in the beginning, but eventually, they drag you down and hold you there. Paul refers to them as "the fleeting pleasures of sin" (Hebrews 11:25). Fleeting is right. I am a reformed two-pack-a-day smoker. I know what I'm talking about. Smoking was so much sneaky fun at first, but was followed by the frustration of many failed attempts to quit, which was not fun at all. Finally breaking decades of bondage to my smoking habit was the most difficult thing I've ever done, and I did not do it alone. God set me free from smoking. And He can free you too.

Almost anyone can relate to the concept of "fleeting pleasure." Who hasn't indulged in too many bowls (or half gallons) of ice cream over the weekend, only to spend the entire next week at the gym trying to undo them?[14] It's fleeting pleasure for sure.

Romans 2:4 says that God's "kindness is intended to turn you away from your sin." God is not a killjoy. He's the opposite. He's the author of joy. His whole problem with sin is that it's destructive, and it takes your freedom. Bondage to sin is what kills joy. So God sent Jesus to win it back for you. "He has sent me ... to proclaim freedom for the captives and release from darkness for the prisoners" (Isaiah 61:1 NIV).

You may be saying, "Well, that's great. Good for you, quitting smoking. But you have no idea how bad it is over here." Listen. No

---

14. I may or may not have familiarity with this absurd cycle.

matter what's going on, it's not too big for the Lord. I mean, He *did* raise Jesus from the dead. He's not intimidated by any hole you can dig yourself into. Counterintuitive as it may sound, you're in a good spot. Maybe not a favorite spot, but a transforming one. There is someone with easy power in your helplessness. The Lord says, "My grace is all you need. My power works best in weakness" (2 Corinthians 12:9). When you've exhausted your own abilities, and nobody else is either able or willing to help, God is. He is both able and willing. All you have to do is ask.

Our Heavenly Father is moved with compassion by our struggles and has the power to free us. But we have a responsibility. We have to make a decision to turn away from the destruction and toward God. Everybody has free will. You have to make the choice for yourself. When I quit smoking, I had to distance myself from the people and places that would suck me back into my smoking habit, at least for a time. Instead of hanging out in the familiar, I spent time building my relationship with God by reading my Bible and talking to Him in prayer. In other words, I repented. Repentance is just stopping what you're doing, then turning and going in a new direction. The word has such a negative connotation. It's been shouted by too many well-meaning preachers. But God is not yelling. He's kindly offering to unhook the leash and set you free.

Of course, there are situations not of our making that leave us bound, unable to move forward. Be encouraged. God frees from sin. All sin. He can restore you from somebody else's sin that has had a crushing effect on your life. He can free you even if that person is never sorry. Just as I released Sailor from Sugarbell's grip, God can release you. Turn towards Him. It may not be instantaneous, but the Lord will free you. The Bible promises that, "The Lord hears His people when they call to Him for help and He rescues them from all their troubles" (Psalm 34:17).

Ask anyone who has been following God for a long time and, without a doubt, they have a rescue story. And you will too.

He drew me up from the pit of destruction, out of the miry bog, and set my feet upon a rock, making my steps secure.

PSALM 40:2 ESV

The Point

Jesus is able and willing to set you free,
but it's your choice.

Journal Prompts

* Has something that you thought would be fun become a burden?
* Do you ever feel like something outside of you controls you?
* What do you think about the word "repentance"?
* What can you do to let God set you free?

Let's Pray

Lord, in every difficulty, You are my banner of victory. You are Jehovah-Nissi, my hope, my freedom. Thank You that You are willing to free me from everything that holds me down and that You can release me from every torment that has any control in my life. Please help me to repent. I'm sorry for the sin in my life. I want to go in a new direction. Show me the steps I can take to live in Your freedom.

To Play

"One Step" by Unspoken

Bark and Keep On Barking

> The LORD is close to all who call on him, yes,
> to all who call on him in truth. He grants
> the desires of those who fear him; he hears
> their cries for help and rescues them.
>
> **PSALM 145:18-19**

Isn't it funny how the things that drive you craziest about someone are things you miss after they're gone? Well, Sailor had this wonderful habit of saying hello to us in the middle of the night. It drove us crazy.

Imagine, if you will, it's 3 a.m. and everyone is sound asleep. Suddenly, we're jolted awake by a single sharp bark, a quick "Hey!" in dog speak. We would try to ignore him, but as soon as we started to drift off again, another yelp, like a smoke alarm's incessant reminder of a low battery. I developed the gift of sleeping right through it; Jeff did not. A shove and a warm suggestion to "go see what your stupid dog wants" was the usual prompt from my adoring husband. Begrudgingly, I'd slide out of bed, drag myself down the stairs, and open the door to find Sailor standing in the middle of the kitchen, tail wagging, thrilled to see me. The sentiment was not mutual.

Any dog trainer will tell you not to reward unwanted behavior. We knew that going downstairs and giving him attention would only encourage him to make this middle-of-the-night hello a habit, but the alternative was to let him bark. All night long. For the record, I was all for ignoring him, though I admit it wasn't easy to hear Sailor's friendly "hello" transition to shrill panic if he didn't get a response. Jeff was not having it. You can't imagine how many minutes of our lives Jeff and I lost lying in bed bickering about whether or not one of us should see what the dog wants, and if so, who. This was one of many opportunities to choose being married over being right.[15] So we took turns seeing what the dog wanted.

Sailor had a range of reasons for summoning us. Occasionally, it was because he needed to go out. Good boy! Sometimes, it was because he overshot the pee pad and thought we might want to go ahead and clean that up. He'd walk me over to it, look at it, look at me, look at it, then go back to bed. I had my orders. Mostly, though, Sailor barked because he missed us. Almost always as soon as I opened the door, he'd greet me with his usual cheer, then turn and click his way across the kitchen back to his bed, glancing behind to make certain I was following. Once at his crate he would plop back into bed with a contented sigh and close his eyes. He had woken up in the middle of the night and now wanted me to tuck him back in! It was as if he was saying, "Hey, I got up, but I'm going back to bed now. Goodnight." Or maybe he just wanted to know we were still there, even when he couldn't see us. I don't know, but it was infuriatingly adorable.

In retrospect, this was the sweetest little habit. I'd like to think that I always patiently patted his fluffy head, pulled his blanket up, and cooed softly to him as he drifted off, knowing how deeply loved

---

15. Though I was right, of course.

he was. But let's be real; 3 a.m. is not the time I'm in full grasp of my blessings. As often as not, I emphatically declared my disapproval of this sleep-crushing idiosyncrasy, only to be met with a single eye opening and a brief wag of the tail as he fell asleep..

I wonder if he ever thought to himself that perhaps he should not bother me, that I wouldn't care about his loneliness or insecurity. Probably not. He had faith in me. He never doubted that I would come and care for him. He could bark for hours and never lose hope that I was going to answer. He just kept barking. And he was right. I always answered eventually.

After he died, his 3 a.m. hello was one of the things I missed most. When I woke in the middle of the night to nothing but silence his absence was profound. No nail clicks on the

Who can stay mad at this guy?

floor, no shrill yip, no one missing me in the middle of the night. He's the only dog I've ever had that was consistently delighted to see me. Every time I looked at him or said his name, his tail would wag. If I left the room, he followed. Our adoration was mutual. Most of the time.

Even without Sailor around to wake me, I'm still up in the middle of the night, sometimes, with little worries zipping around my brain. Rarely does what keeps me awake have gravitas. No sleeplessness over melting icebergs for me. I like to save my insomniac concerns for something truly important like did I remember to make a note on the brunch reservation not to seat us next to the bathrooms. I glance at the clock. It's 3 a.m. Why am I awake? This does not warrant middle-of-the-night problem-solving.

It's funny how Sailor could turn so trustingly to me, a grumpy human, for comfort, while I hesitate to bring my own worries to God, who is self-described as "our refuge and strength, an ever-present help in times of trouble" (Psalm 46:1 BSB). Why would I not follow Sailor's example and invite God into my own 3 a.m. experience? If I truly believe He is the source of peace, why would I not ask for His help? I'll tell you why: because, unlike Sailor, I sometimes, deep in my heart, think that perhaps I am bothering God. Legitimately important things are happening in the world right now. Have you seen the news? God does not want to hear about my trivial problems. My silly, overactive brain does not warrant intervention by the Great I Am. He's busy!

This is simply not true. God does not see me or my middle-of-the-night anxieties, even about dinner reservations, as annoying or insignificant. Look at these words of Jesus:

> *I tell you not to worry about your life. Don't worry about having something to eat, drink, or wear. Isn't life more than food or clothing? Look at the birds in the sky! They don't plant or harvest. They don't even store grain in barns. Yet your Father in heaven takes care of them. Aren't you worth much more than birds?*
>
> *Can worry make you live longer? Why worry about clothes? Look how the wild flowers grow. They don't work hard to make their clothes. But I tell you that Solomon with all his wealth wasn't as well clothed as one of them. God gives such beauty to everything that grows in the fields, even though it is here today and thrown into a fire tomorrow. God will surely do even more for you! Why do you have such little faith?*
>
> *Don't worry and ask yourselves, "Will we have anything to eat? Will we have anything to drink? Will we have*

> any clothes to wear?" Only people who don't know God are always worrying about such things. Your Father in heaven knows you need all of these. But more than anything else, put God's work first and do what he wants. Then the other things will be yours as well.
>
> **MATTHEW 6:25-34** CEV

That doesn't sound like someone who wants you to handle things yourself and leave Him alone. That sounds like someone who wants to assure you that He understands all of your concerns, no matter how small, and is committed to taking care of them and you.

Wouldn't it be good to be like Sailor, full of faith, always trusting I would answer, even when he had to bark and keep on barking? He never worried about bothering me. He never doubted that I would answer. He fully expected me to show up and take care of his needs. He just made his case and waited.

I admit I was sometimes bothered by Sailor's neediness, but can I tell you how much I would love to hear him call for me to tuck him in one more time? Fortunately for us, God doesn't need hindsight to know how precious it is when one of his children calls out for Him. You are never a bother to God. People may get weary, but God never does. You are not on His nerves. He is not worn out with your prayers. He is never too busy, never annoyed, never sleeping, even at 3 a.m.

> And so I tell you, keep on asking, and you will receive what you ask for. Keep on seeking, and you will find. Keep on knocking, and the door will be opened to you.
>
> **LUKE 11:9**

The Point

God wants us to call on Him whenever we need Him.

Journal Prompts

- When was a time you felt worried or alone?
- Do you ever feel like you're bothering God when you talk to Him?
- When you read Matthew 6:25–34, how do you think God views your concerns?
- If someone you loved was upset about something you could easily take care of, what would you want them to do?

Let's Pray

Lord, thank You that You are Jehovah-Shammah, "The Lord is There." Thank You for always being patient and kind when I call on You. I'm sorry for doubting Your availability and doubting my importance to You. Please help me to bring all of my concerns to You. Thank you for caring about the small details of my life.

To Play

"Right on Time" by Aaron Cole

A Crevasse Named Desire

You open your hand and satisfy the desires of every living thing.
PSALM 145:16 NIV

You should see the dogs watch me eat chicken. The longing, the desire. It is immense. Sailor comically monitors the floor, shivering with anticipation, audibly quaking with every exhale. You know the way little kids who've had too much candy ball their fists in front of their faces, clench their teeth, and vibrate in a crazed sugar rush? Do that. Now simultaneously say "uhhhh, uhhhh, uhhhh" under your breath. This is a close approximation to Sailor's audible response to grilled chicken.

As I finish my plate, he's on high alert, body bristled, ready to race for any crumb. You have to admire his optimism. He can barely find a treat that's right in front of him. There's no way he's beating the younger dogs to anything that falls accidentally. Happily for him, I see his hope, know his limitations, love him completely, and will provide for him intentionally, not by accident. He's not getting a stray crumb. He's getting the good stuff. I call his name, lean down, and let the heavenly, smoky scent of grilled chicken invite him to eat from my hand. No chance of interception by the other dogs. No competition.

Can anyone else relate to near-obsessive desire, maybe not for chicken, but for something? Ours is a culture of side hustles and *carpe diem*. We're consumed with seizing the day and getting what's ours. Ugh. The expectation that every day of one's life should be remarkable is ridiculous. Some days are grocery days. Those days do not feel adequately seized. Who needs the pressure of feeling like a failure because the only thing you carpe'd today was produce and canned goods? The overemphasis on curating an extraordinary (and more currently, an Instagramable) life has driven us into a bottomless crevasse of unquenchable desire.

Just for fun, let's dip into what the "more" we want is. What's the stuff we could easily fall into near-obsession over if we weren't the bastions of contentment that we aspire to be? I'll go first.

Appreciation

I want somebody to say "Hey, good job!" Right now, my main responsibility in life is taking care of my family. I am a stay-at-home mom or, in other decades, a "housewife." Cringe. The career-driven 28-year-old me cannot even believe what she's seeing. She thought staying at home was for people who wanted to watch Oprah and iron all day. She would never in a million years do that.[16]

---

[16]. A brief aside: I kid you not, Jeff and I married in Jamaica two weeks after I quit my job and moved to Illinois to get married. Prior to those two weeks, I had worked at least one and up to three jobs at all times since I was 16 years old. The questionnaire I had to fill out for the Jamaican marriage certificate asked about my age, previous marital status, and current job title (34; single; none). To my horror, when I received the final official marriage certificate (the legal one that you have to present to acquire things like passports), they had written my profession as "house duties" and my status as "spinster." Yes, they did. I almost died. But they were eerily prophetic, because "house duties" has indeed been an accurate descriptor for the last sixteen years of married parenthood. A pic is posted on my instagram for your amusement. instagram.com/leslievicary/

It's so easy to feel insignificant when you no longer have a paycheck or a job title to affirm your worth. I have to remind myself that for now, my number one assignment is taking care of the people who have been entrusted to me, and that job is as important as anything else I am going to do in this lifetime.

Let me just stop here and say that if you're a caretaker of any sort, you're valuable. The people you serve will likely never fully comprehend the sacrifices you make on their behalf, but God sees you, and He thinks what you're doing is of utmost importance. In fact, His number two commandment is "Love others," right behind "Love the Lord your God" (Matthew 27:37–39). Putting your own desires on hold to take care of another person is most certainly loving others. So, hey, good job!

And speaking of affirming oneself, here's the best bit of advice I ever learned from a preschooler: self-congratulations. It can save your whole day.

At the end of a very long half-day in the two-year-old preschool room, we grownups encouraged the herd of tiny humans to help put the toys away. Predictably futile. May-May, however, was all in. She was dressed in upscale Charleston toddler attire, a smocked dress with hand-embroidered sailboats around the collar and a bow three times the size of her head. It gave her the same old-money aristocracy vibe as men who wear seersucker suits and wraparound sport sunglasses simultaneously on Easter Sunday.

No slacker, May-May would pick up a single block, carry it all the way across the room, throw it in the block bin, clap her hands, and exclaim: "Good job, May May!" Then she'd bounce back across the room to do it again, applauding herself every time. She wasn't waiting for somebody else to cheer her contribution! She knew her worth! This continued, one block at a time, until she moved the whole stack across the room, into the block bin.

May-May is not even my name, but to this day, I clap my hands and say to myself, "Good job, May-May!" when I do something impressive like patiently smiling when someone declares "There's nothing to eat!" after I spent an entire day of my life seizing groceries. Know your contribution and applaud it even when no one else does. But back to the list of near obsessions.

Cash, Baby

Right after appreciation, or maybe before, I would like cash. I am aware that by sheer virtue of living in the United States, I am among the wealthiest humans on the planet and incredibly blessed. But can I be honest? If you get me started on all I would like to have and do, we could be here for a while. Contentment is a skill that I am still in the process of cultivating. To that end, I spent a whole boatless summer[17] taking long, hot walks, and meditating on Psalm 16. None of this material stuff is going to last anyway, and I should focus on things that matter for eternity. Moth and rust inevitably ruin everything (Matthew 6:19 paraphrase mine). Yes. Got it. I am on board. But since we're talking about getting on board, let me just tell you what I'd do with more money than I could shake a stick at: travel.

Back when we had a boat and the dogs looked like luggage in their life vests.

---

17. We had a boat! Then we sold it, the pain of which was right up there with trading the Miata for a sensible four-door.

I have a friend who has become so accustomed to her fabulous lifestyle that she makes casual, off-hand references to her weekend on the boat (read *yacht*) of some bazillionaire. She's not even intentionally name-dropping or yacht-dropping or whatever you want to call it. It's just her life.

Meanwhile, I'm hoping my husband and I will finally take that trip up the Mediterranean coast we planned for our tenth anniversary. We've postponed so many times that we'll be lucky to get there for our twenty-fifth. One of the main reasons I originally wanted to go was to live out this fantasy of biking through wine country on a path with a view of the Mediterranean Sea on one side and grape-covered hills on the other. (Hey, I've seen romcoms.) The sad thing is that now every time I ride a bike, my knees hurt. At this point, I just want to get to Italy before I have to trade my bicycle for a Little Rascal with seat lift.

Accomplishment

Oh, boy. This is a book in itself. There are certain career avenues that I have pursued for years with stunningly little success. Doors have opened that I failed to walk through; doors have closed for unknown reasons. Life choices (aka house duties) have impeded progress. And throughout this maddeningly slow march, I have watched peers who started the pursuit long after I did rapidly move forward. It is not an easy experience. Comparison is an emotional Chutes and Ladders slide that always dumps you back on square one, "Sad Pit of Discontent."

It can be so challenging to be happy for the success of others while it eludes me. But I know this: God's in charge, and God loves me. I truly believe that all of His plans for me are good, so if I'm not getting what I want, then not having it is to my benefit, at least for now. Trusting God is essential. It's the quickest rope up and out of the Sad Pit of Discontent.

This is a short list and doesn't even include material things.[18] We are swamped with messages enticing us to desire more of everything. Our culture tells us that if we're not having these lavish, cinematic experiences, we can't be content. Culture tells us that to be happy, we need more flashy things. Culture tells us that if we haven't achieved a certain income or certain dress size, we are substandard. And yet there are a lot of rich, famous, fit, miserable people running around out there. Culture doesn't know what it's talking about. God knows what He's talking about. He designed us. He knows what makes us truly content, even when we don't.

Think back to the story of Joseph in chapter one. Imagine his frustration at being human trafficked by his own brothers, while they remained free. Imagine remaining unjustly imprisoned as he watched others be released. His faith is literally legendary. Joseph chose to believe that God was in control and that whatever happened was for his ultimate good. And it was. "God intended it all for good" (Genesis 50:20). You and I get to make the same choice to trust or not. It may take time, but we will eventually see His goodness.

If I just zoom out for a minute and look at the context of my overall life, I can better understand God's POV. Let's go back to my unrequited aspirations. When I look through the lens of what I do have rather than what I do not, I can see that God has not been oblivious to my struggle. He has been kind.

Instead of spending extremely long days and weeks away from home, working in an industry that will still be here in ten years, I have spent those days being an irreplaceable part of my daughter's

---

18. Don't get me started on deck boats.

young life. Her childhood will not be here in ten years. It's like a sunrise, magnificent and unrepeatable. If I miss it, I will have missed it. I can't even imagine the pain of that realization after the opportunity has passed. Being part of Eden's story is the best part of my story and the greatest blessing of my life. Missing that would have been my greatest regret. God has not been dismissive of my desires. He has been merciful. He has given me the true desire of my heart, the one I didn't even know to ask for.

Much like Sailor, lurching to catch a stray crust, I have often missed what I strive for, but I have gotten something better. God sees my hope, knows my limitations, loves me completely, and provides for me intentionally, not by accident. He calls me by name and opens His hand.

How wonderful are your gifts to me; how good they are!

PSALM 16:6 GNT

The Point
We can trust God.

Journal Prompts
- What are some things you could fall into near-obsessive desire over?
- When do you find it difficult to be content?
- How do you feel about seizing the day *and* grocery days?
- Where can you see that God has withheld something you hoped for, but given something better?

Let's Pray
Father God, you are Jehovah-Jireh, the Lord who provides. You give more than enough. Thank You for providing all I need and for blessing me with beautiful things I don't even know to ask for. Thank You for contentment and peace that only comes from You. I'm sorry for the times when I'm discontented. Please help me to recognize Your goodness and protection. Help me to live with gratitude for all of Your blessings in my life.

To Play
"The Goodness of God" by Bethel Worship

A Miserable Mess

Turn to me and be gracious to me, for I am lonely and afflicted. The troubles of my heart have multiplied; free me from my anguish. Look upon my affliction and my distress and take away all my sins.

PSALM 25:16–18 NIV

In life, you will let go of things that are painful to lose, but more painful to keep. For Sailor, it was several of his teeth. Perhaps you are a wonderful dog owner who has mastered the brushing of your dog's teeth. We were not. We had used water additives and dental chews but, alas, it was not enough, as illustrated by Sailor's unbearable breath. It was brutal. He already had the mouth noise and licking going; now there was his breath. At the time we just chalked it up to "dog breath." But in the end, it came down to letting him have the couch to himself forevermore or getting him some professional help.

Does anyone else remember the '80s when dogs stayed outside, ate Gravy Train, got their rabies shots once a year, and you were done? Those were heady, low-maintenance times, my friend. Not so today. Case in point: dental visits. We were surprised to learn that now you're expected to have your dog's teeth cleaned annually. I know people who don't get their own teeth cleaned annually, much less their dogs! This would have been considered preposterous back in the '80s.[19]

The doggie dental appointment is not your simple 30-minute trip to the dentist. The last time we had our dogs' teeth cleaned it was about $400 per dog. Per dog! It's a huge, expensive deal, complete with bloodwork, anesthesia, and an all-day appointment. Turns out, dogs won't just lie there peacefully letting some stranger scrape their teeth. So they put them to sleep. If only I could find a dentist who would do the same for me.

We signed Sailor up for his first cleaning, ordered the required bloodwork—and second mortgages—and dropped him off. When I returned for him that afternoon, I was aghast to learn that a couple of his teeth had been extracted. They don't fill them; they just pull them. What we thought was part of Sailor's identity as a dog (e.g., dog breath) was actually a symptom of infirmity. We had no idea. Worst dog mom of the year right here. Fortunately, our vet knew exactly how to help him, even though it was not a pleasant process for any of us.

Just as we treated Sailor's symptom like a character trait, sometimes people treat foul symptoms like anger or anxiety, as if they are character traits rather than symptoms. This leads to a terrible misconception that says "This is just who I am." Our self-perception is distorted like a fun-room mirror and we believe that a sign of infirmity is our identity. Let me straighten that warped reflection out for you right now. "Angry" is not who you are. "Anxious" is not who you are. "Depressed" is not who you are. You were never created to be any of those things. They are temporary states. You may *feel* anxious or depressed or angry. That does not make it your identity. These are just signs that there's a wound that hasn't healed. Yet.

---

19. It is not lost on me how old that sentence makes me sound. "Back in the good ole days when bread cost a dime and women didn't wear pants." And by that I mean they wore skirts.

When other people harm us, intentionally or not, or when we harm ourselves, intentionally or not, an emotional wound results. If it's not treated, that pain will shape our beliefs and choices until it infects our entire lives. The Bible calls that lingering wound a poisonous root of bitterness that grows up to trouble you (see Hebrews 12:15). Have you ever been called "bitter"? It's usually said with rude accusation, which literally adds insult to injury. But the bitterness is born of pain. It's nothing that warrants an insult. It warrants tender care. Let me assure you that God isn't criticizing you. He knows how bitterness happens and He wants to make you whole. And the only way to be whole is to get healing for those old injuries.

Here we are giving him cookies and ruining his teeth.
Just kidding! It's a dog treat.

You have a compassionate Savior "who redeems your life from the pit and crowns you with love and compassion" (Psalm 103:4 NIV). Jesus died so that all of your hurts can be healed, physically and emotionally. He knows the festering wound and how to treat it. He knows the loop playing in your brain and how to break it.

If you look up the word "redeem," it means to *set free from what distresses or harms*. If you allow Him into your life, Jesus is going to redeem you, freeing you from what distresses you, by cleaning some things up and extracting other things completely. He's not just going to leave you to your misery. He has a good purpose for you. Listen to the words of Almighty God. "'For I know the plans I have for you,' declares the LORD, 'plans to prosper you and not to harm you, plans to give you hope and a future. Then you will call on me and come and pray to me, and I will listen to you. You will seek me and find me when you seek me with all your heart. I will be found by you,' declares the LORD, 'and will bring you back from captivity'" (Jeremiah 29:11–14 NIV).

Jesus Christ died for us, not only to cover our sins but to deliver us from every evil thing humans endure: guilt, shame, disease, depression, anxiety, addiction, abuse, poverty—you name it. In Christ, we have the power to overcome everything that torments us. He is able to heal, to free, and to restore you—if you are willing to receive it.

Losing some things from your life, even hurtful things, might sound scary. But let me assure you that for everything you lose, something so much better will be left in its place. Isaiah 61:1–3 is Jesus's beautiful promise "to bind up the brokenhearted, to proclaim freedom for the captives... to bestow... beauty instead of ashes, joy instead of mourning." I'll take it.

The Spirit of the Sovereign Lord is on me,
   because the Lord has anointed me
   to proclaim good news to the poor.
He has sent me to bind up the brokenhearted,
   to proclaim freedom for the captives
   and release from darkness for the prisoners,
to proclaim the year of the Lord's favor
   and the day of vengeance of our God,
to comfort all who mourn,
   and provide for those who grieve in Zion—
to bestow on them a crown of beauty
   instead of ashes,
the oil of joy
   instead of mourning,
and a garment of praise
   instead of a spirit of despair.
They will be called oaks of righteousness,
   a planting of the Lord
   for the display of his splendor.

ISAIAH 61:1–3 NIV

The Point

With God, some losses are actually gains.

Journal Prompts

- What has been painful to lose that you're better off without?
- Have you ever believed that a symptom of a wound (anger, depression, etc.) was your identity?
- Do you still suffer from old emotional wounds that haven't been fully healed?
- How do you think the word "redeem" relates to you?

Let's Pray

Jehovah-Rophe, You are the Lord who Heals. Thank You, Jesus, for dying for me. Thank You for overcoming every physical and emotional affliction. Please redeem me and set me free from old hurts. Help me to forgive people, even when they aren't sorry. Help me to release the pain to You, so You can heal me and show me my true identity in You. Thank you for replacing despair and mourning with freedom and joy.

To Play

"Come to the Altar" by Elevation Worship

I'm Not Here

Nothing in all creation is hidden from God's sight.

HEBREWS 4:13 NIV

There is a feral cat who lives in the storm drain in front of our house. She rises from the underground to sit in the middle of the road, just beyond the reach of our dogs, where she provocatively twitches her tail back and forth, mocking them. She mercilessly antagonizes them with her bedraggled presence. You can imagine how much Sailor enjoys sitting in the grass as close to the underground fence zap zone as possible, barking endlessly at this cat.

A word about the location of this barkfest. Our house is at the end of a cul-de-sac, which gives us a lovely view of asphalt from our front window, so I planted a privacy screen of shrubbery. Among the shrubs is a path of stones just wide enough for our dogs to cross through the bed to a strip of grass on the other side. This was Sailor's favorite place to lounge, close enough to the street that people walking past might stop to pet him as well as a prime spot to participate in his daily feud with the cat.

A scenario: I am working in the home office. I hear Sailor bark. And bark. And bark. I hope Ms. Feral grows weary of her taunting and decides to take her torment elsewhere. Alas, she does not. She flips her tail with a superior, bored demeanor as usual. The barking continues as usual. I sigh, leave my project, go to the door, and exasperatedly call for Sailor to stop barking. He does not. I call for him to come into the house. No response. I offer treats. Nothing. I entice with chicken, normally a guarantee. But not today.

From behind the leggy branches of an azalea bush, he peers at me, stretches his neck long, ducks his head low, and narrows his gaze. He's hiding. Apparently, Sailor does not notice the total lack of leaves on this stick-plant of an azalea and believes he is fully camouflaged. Even as we enter the stare down phase of our standoff, it doesn't register that I can see him. Bless it.

"Sailor, come in here," I say, this time low voiced, eyebrows pointedly raised. He remains frozen. "You want some chicken? Chicken!" His tail swishes involuntarily. He's a study in conflicting desires but continues to hide behind the azalea as if he cannot hear me. "Sailor, I see you looking at me. You're behind the bush. Come here!" I stand there on the porch in my pajamas, negotiating with a dog who believes he's invisible for much longer than I should probably admit.

Until I walk halfway across the yard through damp grass, getting the bottom of my pajama pants soaked, he does not budge. Finally, when I am within arm's reach from him, he realizes I'm onto his game and steps out from behind the azalea, tail wagging. Again, a study in conflict. Is he glad to see me or disappointed to be found? He doesn't know. I scoop him up and carry him back to the house while gently urging him to ignore the taunts of that mangy cat. He is far too good for her.

Even though I had to walk out and physically pick him up to bring him back to me, even though he was disobedient, even though he hid from me, he still got his treats.[20] I wasn't mad at him. I understood him.

---

20. An affront to proper dog training.

Invisible to the human eye.

Sailor's hiding habit came to mind as my daughter and I were reading the story of Sarah in Genesis 18. God tells the elderly Abraham that he and his wife will finally have a baby. Not only will they have a baby, but they will have many descendants, too numerous to count, through which God will bless the whole world.

Keep in mind that Abraham was almost a hundred years old and Sarah was also old and "long past the age of having children" (Genesis 18:11). It was too late for her. In a culture where children were considered one's greatest asset, I'm sure that being childless left her feeling inadequate. "Barren" doesn't even sound like a word to describe a human, but a terrain, and yet this was the depressing lens through which the world saw her and she likely saw herself.

While Abraham was being told of this coming baby, we find Sarah hiding just inside her tent, eavesdropping on the whole conversation. She "laughed silently to herself and said, 'how could a worn-out woman like me enjoy such pleasure, especially when my master—my husband—is also so old'" (Genesis 18:12). I'm going to go out on a limb and say Sarah was bitter. Who wouldn't be cynical at this announcement? What she longed for her entire life was finally fulfilled—when she was ninety.

As far as child-bearing goes, Sarah was looking at two possible scenarios. Worst case, she'll die barren, as I'm sure she assumed she would. Best case, she'll be the old lady with a baby. Had there been a *Star* magazine, she would have been on the cover under the "Geriatric Mom Has Miracle Baby" headline. Not preferable. Gratitude seems like a stretch.

God, knowing everything, as He does, hears her behind the tent flap and asks why she laughed. Incite panic. I mean, you're cold-busted, laughing sarcastically at God Almighty's plan to create a nation for Himself through you and your ancient uterus. This is next level turning around to find the person you're trash-talking standing right behind you. So Sarah does what any good guilty person would do. Deny. Deny. Deny. Sarah and God have a back and forth about whether she laughed or not. Then she hides from him.

Reading that, my young daughter exclaimed with amusement: "You can't hide from God, lady! He knows you're there!" She's right. We're not pulling anything over on God. He knows everything about us, including our best hiding places. He sees right through those tent flaps and azalea bushes. Sarah's childlessness and humiliation were not news to God. Her laughter wasn't going to throw Him off His plan or incur His wrath. He looks with compassion on our humanity, so easily taunted and shamed. When He calls us out of hiding, it is always with love, never with condemnation.

About a year later Sarah laughed again, and that time, gratitude really was her response!

> Now the LORD was gracious to Sarah as he had said and the LORD did for Sarah what he had promised. Sarah became pregnant and bore a son to Abraham in his old age,

*at the very time God had promised him....
Sarah said, "God has brought me laughter,
and everyone who hears about this will
laugh with me... Who would have said to
Abraham that Sarah would nurse children?
Yet I have borne him a son in his old age."*

GENESIS 21:1–2, 6–7 NIV

You can read the entire account of Sarah in Genesis, chapters 15–18 and 21. She made some major mistakes attempting to solve her own childlessness, but God was gracious. Despite her hiding, her dishonesty, and her mistakes, God treated her with kindness. He understood her. And she still got her prize (a baby!).

God knows where you are, physically and emotionally. And He's not mad at you. He understands you. Even when you resist, God is still there, holding your blessing in His hand, if you only choose to come out and receive it.

*O LORD, you have examined my heart
and know everything about me.
You know when I sit down or stand up.
You know my thoughts even when I'm far away.
You see me when I travel
and when I rest at home.
You know everything I do.
You know what I am going to say
even before I say it, Lord.
You go before me and follow me.
You place your hand of blessing on my head.*

PSALM 139:1–5

The Point

God knows everything about you,
and He ain't mad atcha.

Journal Prompts

- When have you felt a need to hide from someone in authority?
- What happened when you came clean (or were dragged out)?
- How do you feel about God knowing everything about you?
- What do you think of God understanding our faults but still blessing us?

Let's Pray

Lord, You are the God who sees me, El Roi. Thank You for knowing my struggles and understanding me. Forgive me for the times I hide from You or avoid You. Please help me to be honest with You and to believe that You aren't mad at me or judging me harshly. Thank You for blessing me when I don't deserve it.

To Play

"Known" by Tauren Wells

Yard Full of Lard

*Make me walk along the path of
your commands, for that is where
my happiness is found.*

PSALM 119:35

The delivery truck goes so ludicrously fast through our neighborhood that I'm afraid for Sailor's sweet, precious life. It careens around corners with a distinctly *Mad Max* post-apocalyptic vibe. It's ridiculous.

So great was my concern for Sailor and for the little ladies frequently out walking their dogs, that I flagged the driver down and very politely asked him to drive more slowly. I pointed out the unlikeliness of anyone being able to leap out of the path of his truck as it hurtled down the street. Politeness wasted. Second step: call the company. And can I just say that few things in life make you feel more like a full on senior citizen than calling a company to complain about a fast driver? And all for nothing. Despite my sacrifice of pride, nothing changed.

Contrast this with our UPS guy. He actually slows down when he passes our home. Slows down! Once, when he was delivering a package, I expressed my appreciation for his conscientious driving (again, feeling like a full-on senior citizen). Do you know what he said to me? He said that he slows down intentionally because he knows I have small dogs who are often in the yard near the street. How much warmth swelled in my heart for our UPS man? Plenty.[21]

All this blue-hair persnicketiness over fast drivers was caused by one thing: Sailor. He's half-deaf, oblivious to traffic, and intoxicated by whatever is underneath the leaves in our neighbor's backyard. We have a sweet neighbor who loves all living creatures. She feeds the birds. And the bees. And the ants. And the feral cats. And whatever else eats. I've heard chunks of suet are thrown out in the yard for the squirrels. Whatever it is, there's something under those leaves, and my baby dog is powerless to resist it.

Sailor and Sugarbell have, on occasion, discovered the serendipity of a faded battery in their Invisible Fence collars and taken off to explore the neighborhood, much to my panic. But usually, if they're not in our yard, I can just look across the street and find them. There, in a sea of rotting brown leaves, is a puff of white, my sainted Sailor, eating a chunk of dirt-covered lard.

The siren lure of a yard full of lard coupled with a careening delivery truck created a perfect dead-dog-in-the-road storm in my mind. My imagination saw Sailor, gasping for his last breath as I held his limp body in my arms, shaking my one free fist against fast drivers and suet suppliers everywhere.

Sailor—God love him—is not the spritely lad of his past. If he wanders out into the street, it takes a lot for him to jump the curb back into our yard. It's as if his brain gives the command to move, then his body says, "One Mississippi, two Mississippi..." before springing forward so spasmodically that it almost knocks him over.

---

21. UPS, I see you and I'm thumping my chest twice and making a peace sign at you.

He's also a little deaf. I think. It's possible that he just ignores me. But whether it's deafness, lack of dexterity, or both, let's just say he's the dog most likely to be standing dumbstruck in the middle of the road with a delivery truck screaming straight for him.

The only tool I have at my disposal to protect my sweet, sainted baby from certain death is his Invisible Fence collar. If you're unfamiliar with these, it's a collar that coordinates with an underground fence to give a harmless, though undesirable, electrical zap if he crosses it. I committed to making sure his collar was on him every single time he went outside, fastening it securely, making sure the prongs rested snugly against his neck for maximum skin-to-zap deterrence. Sailor's collar is so tight it's a wonder that I don't choke him out and accidentally kill him myself.

I don't enjoy making him wear the collar or seeing him get zapped. The ideal scenario would be for him to stay in the safety of our yard out of sheer obedience, but I know Sailor well enough to know that he is never going to be able to resist the lure of yard lard.

How many times has God said a similar thing about me? I can hear Him now. "I know Leslie well enough to know that she is never going to be able to resist the lure of winning this argument." I do like to stay in the argument until I am fully (and sometimes way too loudly) heard. In my natural state, I cannot resist trying to convince the other person (Jeff) that I am right. I will not stop until one of our sides (his) is dead on the floor like a sad little mound of relationship roadkill.

If there was a Mixed Martial Arts for arguments, I would have finally found a sport in which I could excel. And all my fellow MMA arguers can give a good amen that it is not a happy championship. The only thing more miserable than winning an argument with your spouse at 1 a.m. is winning it while camping in the rain.

God knows I need boundaries to keep from crossing into territory that is enticing but destructive. "Being right" wins arguments, but loses things like marriages. God is not a fan. He doesn't want me to be a person who refuses to see a new perspective and sometimes concedes that I am (gasp!) wrong. He also doesn't want me to be a doormat with no voice. There's a happy medium. You can treat other people like you want to be treated, even in disagreements. Hold on. That sounds familiar. Why that's the Golden Rule! "So in everything, do to others what you would have them do to you" (Matthew 7:12 NIV). Such a simple guideline. But easier said than done. Am I right?

God's boundaries are designed to protect us and those who have to be around us from harm. Fortunately God does not operate in zap collars. He operates in the Holy Spirit. The Holy Spirit—described as a comforter, friend, and helper—warns us when we're getting too close to the edge, oblivious to the dangers careening towards us. God has given us rules to guide us, not to ruin our fun, but to keep us safe. He's not leaving us to ourselves. And that's a good thing.

I keep Sailor within the fence because I am aware of hazards that he knows nothing about. Besides getting run over by a delivery truck, let's talk about eating unlimited amounts of lard for a minute. He is blissfully unaware of the possible repercussions. Likewise, God knows the hazards we know nothing about. He wants us to obey Him so we can stay out of painful, damaging situations. His intent is for us to live beautiful, healthy lives. He "came that we may have life and have it abundantly" (John 10:10 ESV).

*"Observe what the L*ORD *your God requires: Walk in obedience to him, and keep his decrees and commands, his laws and regulations, as written in the Law of Moses. Do this so that you may prosper in all you do and wherever you go."*

1 KINGS 2:3 NIV

The Point

God's rules are there to protect us
(and everybody else).

Journal Prompts

* How do you generally feel about boundaries and rules?

* What can you not resist? I know_____ well enough to know that he/she is never going to be able to resist the lure of _____.

* How does God help you stay within the boundaries?

* When was a time you've been pulled back into safety (physically, relationally, etc.) by the Holy Spirit?

Let's Pray

Dear Lord, You are Jehovah-M'Kaddesh. You set us apart for Your purposes. Thank You for the Holy Spirit who guides me and warns me. Thank You for setting up clear boundaries to protect me. I'm sorry for the times I jump over the line. Help me to trust that You have reasons for Your rules and to be obedient.

To Play

"Not Gon' Do" by Andy Mineo
(featuring Joseph Solomon)

Whiny Little Man Dog

*Whoever dwells in the shelter of the Most
High will rest in the shadow of the Almighty.
I will say of the L*ORD*, "He is my refuge and
my fortress, my God, in whom I trust."*

PSALM 91:1-2 NIV

Poor little Sailor is so whiny these days. He whines loudly when we're out of the room and softly when we're in the room. It's pitiful. Last week we came home on Christmas Eve to find him walking like a drunk dog. He would stagger, then abruptly sit. Thinking he probably hurt his hip, we kept him quiet through the holiday then took him to the vet on the day after Christmas. We quickly realized that we could be faced with putting him down or paying for expensive back surgery. It was a disc issue. He's old and so is his back. Much credit goes to my wonderful husband for not even needing a second to consider which of these options we would take. If Sailor needed surgery, he would have surgery.

Fortunately, after a ridiculously expensive night in the doggie ER, Sailor was released without surgery. We were given meds to administer, instructions for physical therapy, which consisted of a lot of toe pinching and leg circling, and a strict order to crate rest him for thirty days. Yep, thirty days in a cage. That's a lot of lying around, even for a dog. Now, seven days into his thirty-day sentence he's out of his happy meds, and we are out of our quiet. Poor Sailor whines and cries and barks constantly. Constantly. We perform an infinite cycle of tasks: food-water-toy-meds, food-water-toy-meds. We have no idea what he wants. Nothing ceases the whimpering.

In the end, after much experimentation, let me tell you what finally makes the man dog stop crying: proximity. As I write this, he lounges by my chair in an open crate, head and front feet hanging out, occasionally opening one eye to see if I'm still here. He is finally content, able to rest, knowing I'm on guard. His cries weren't from pain or hunger, but for assurance that his person is close by. It's comforting to have someone looking out for you, especially when you're hurt and tired.

Sailor's need for proximity is not unique. When my toddler was experiencing her wildest throes of ear-splitting despair, the quickest way to quiet her was not to turn up my own volume from across the room, but to come close, eye to eye, her hands in mine, speaking softly as I gave her my full, intimate attention. It's tantrum kryptonite. She'd usually end up in my lap, asleep. This works for adults, too, though it's a little weirder to administer.

Sometimes, we grown-ups are just like big, tired toddlers. So take a nap. It's okay. Let me ask you a question: When you see a dog asleep on their backs with all four feet up in the air, do you get mad? Of course not. Dogs have a limited number of expectations placed on them: eat, go outside, play, and sleep. We don't malign them for taking a nap. We expect them to sleep for most of the day. I have a million photos of my dogs comically napping—on their backs with all paws in the air, with their head in someone's shoe, or wrapped

Like a hat.

around my sleeping husband's head like a hat. They're supposed to sleep. And guess what? You are expected to rest too.

> *Remember to observe the Sabbath day by keeping it holy [set apart]. You have six days each week for your ordinary work, but the seventh day is a Sabbath day of rest dedicated to the LORD your God. On that day no one in your household may do any work.*
> **EXODUS 20:8-10**

Well, isn't that a welcome instruction? God expects us to take a whole day every week just to spend time with Him and rest. Not only is God okay with you taking a load off, He included it in the Ten Commandments. He knows we need a nap.

Of course, sometimes you need more than a nap. Life fatigue can seep deep down into your soul. Do you ever feel like you could be that guy in a western slumped over his horse riding across the desert, who wakes up in some old geezer's run-down cabin four days later? Now that's tired. Life can throw some weight on you that makes you feel like you could sleep for about four days, but God gives rest for soul fatigue, too.

Jesus said, "Come to me, all of you who are weary and carry heavy burdens, and I will give you rest" (Matthew 11:28). Did you notice the first step in this verse is proximity: come close. Just as Sailor needed proximity to me, we need proximity to God. Get where you can experience His presence. I like to go somewhere natural and quiet where I can hear the breeze blowing and birds singing. But God is everywhere, so even if you aren't able to get away from distraction, you can still experience His presence.

Second step: lay it on Him. Give Jesus the emotional burdens you've been dragging around. Ask Him to take what's too much for you. Name it. Out loud. If you want that baggage back later, you can take it back. But for now, see how it feels to be light. You might feel silly but just say: "Jesus, (fill in the blank) is too heavy for me. I'm giving it to You. Now please give me the rest You promised." You can even open your hands to visualize letting your stuff go and receiving rest. Then take a deep breath. The Lord says, "Be still and know that I am God" (Psalm 46:10 NIV). In other words, "Stop doing things. I got you" (paraphrase mine).

Jesus is talking about rest for your worn-out soul, not just about physical sleep, but a good nap is a good place to start. I'm going to cut this short so you can take a minute to lay back and close your eyes, knowing that the Holy Spirit is close by and watching over you. This may sound a little kooky, but I like to imagine myself curling up in the palm of God's hand, knowing that nothing can touch me there. I've been using that image since I was a little girl, and it works. Try it! And if you have somewhere to be, set an alarm. You might need it.

*In peace [and with a tranquil heart] I will both
lie down and sleep, For You alone, O Lord,
make me dwell in safety and confident trust.*

PSALM 4:8 AMP

The Point

Jesus gives rest.

Journal Prompts

- What's the most tired you've ever been?
- Where and when do you most easily focus on the LORD and experience His presence?
- What are grievances or emotional burdens that prevent you from peacefully resting?
- Would you try opening your hand and offering Him these burdens in exchange for rest?

Let's Pray

Jesus, you are Jehovah-Shalom,[22] the LORD our peace. Thank You for being close. Thank You that You aren't frantic or loud, but calm. Thank You for bringing order to my chaos and for bringing wholeness and peace to my life. I'm sorry for not coming to You first when I need a safe place. Please help me experience Your presence. I give my burdens to You.

To Play

"The Name" by Maverick City Music x Kirk Franklin (featuring Brandon Lake & Maryann J. George)

---

22. Here's an easy and fun way to study God's word—Bible Project animated videos. Check this one out. bibleproject.com/explore/video/shalom-peace.

Hornets to Hyenas

"For I know the plans I have for you," declares the LORD "plans to prosper you and not to harm you, plans to give you hope and a future."

JEREMIAH 29:11 NIV

Around here every meal is a study in patient expectation. The dogs form a semicircle at my feet, noses twitching, eyes unblinking. They want what I've got, and I have every intention of giving it to them. Three bites of steak are already lined up at the edge of my plate. They know this. Getting the last bite is an every-meal occurrence. But that doesn't mean they're willing to run the risk of missing their bite by taking their eyes off of me. Sugarbell and Sunflower are focused as runners at a starting block, listening for the final scrapes of the fork while Sailor watches the floor, shivering with his usual comic anticipation.

As one who is woefully prone to distraction, I sometimes forget to share, even with the bites lined up neatly on the side of my plate. I forget that they're reserved for the dogs and eat them myself. In confusion, they watch me get up from the table and head to the kitchen without sharing.

You can see them trying to process what has just happened. They look to me, to each other, to the floor. Sailor lifts a paw like a furry, disappointed question mark. They walk in circles, sniffing the floor, trying to locate what must have been the pieces they failed to see drop. It's so sweet the way they assume the mistake is theirs, not mine.

I wouldn't let them wait with all that hope just to fail them—would I? Of course not. Realizing my error, I am on my way to the kitchen to get more steak, just for them. Their trust is not misplaced. I have not dismissed their desires. They are not being ignored. They are not being punished. They just need to give me a minute.

They're not actually watching me eat here, but this is the look. front to back—Sunflower, Sugarbell, Sailor

See if this sounds familiar. You are expecting something from God. You pray. You work on what you can. You wait. You remind yourself that things happen in His time, not your time. Months (or years) tick by. You are confused. You wonder if you should keep on hoping or give up.

This is a well-traveled road. How often do you hear extremely successful people talk about how many years they spent working toward their dream and how many times they considered quitting before they finally had their breakthrough?

It's tempting to look at other people's achievements and forget that they also struggled. Nobody just arrives. Every single human encounters challenges. But when you're the one facing resistance, it feels like you're the only one. And it's confusing. Why is it so difficult to accomplish something you're certain God prompted you to do? Shouldn't this be easy? Why isn't He helping? What about all the verses saying nothing is too hard for Him, and the earth is the Lord's and everything in it, and if God is for us, who can be against us? What about that?

Wow. Good questions. I should have an answer here.

Actually, why would I have the answer? Why would I think that I can explain the choices of God? That's ridiculous! And presumptuous! Like it says in Isaiah 55:8, "'My thoughts are not like your thoughts,'" says the Lord. "'And my ways are far beyond anything you could imagine.'" Yes, they are.

Fortunately God has given us His Word, the Bible. If I want an answer as to why God does anything, the one source I can trust for truth is the Bible. Everything in it is God-inspired and His favorite tool to reveal Himself to us, so let's take a look.

I bet you never learned this verse in Sunday School.[23] "I will send the hornet ahead of you to drive the Hivites, Canaanites and Hittites out of your way. But I will not drive them out in a single year, because the land would become desolate and the wild animals too numerous for you. Little by little I will drive them out before you, until you have increased enough to take possession of the land" (Exodus 23:28–30 NIV).

God has a big picture, all-knowing, future-seeing perspective that I do not have. If I'm praying for something that He's not giving me, it might not be that I'll never have it. It might be that I have to wait. We've heard the phrase "God's timing" to the point of triteness. I'm

---

[23]. In all the thousands of lessons and sermons I've witnessed, I don't know that I had ever even heard of this verse, then—Bam!— just as I was writing this chapter, it was in the day's Bible Recap. God is talking if you're listening. Reading through the entire Bible is one of the best things I've ever done. There's a lot to be said for not missing a single verse. I highly recommend The Bible Recap. With their plan you read a couple of chapters a day in chronological order—so it's more of a story rather than random Scripture—then you listen to a brief podcast that gives insight into what you just read. Game-changer. www.thebiblerecap.com

sure it's stitched on a pillow and sold in a Hobby Lobby somewhere. But stick with me and let's try to see timing from God's perspective.

First, let us notice that while the people are waiting to take possession of their promised land (aka manifest their dream), God is doing the unenviable work of moving populations of people out of their way. Do you know what they call it when one people group forces another people group out of their land? War. Who wants war? Exactly. Sometimes we're waiting because God is doing us a huge favor. God can get the hard stuff done creatively and without casualty. We're just so focused on achieving the end result that we don't see the delay as the blessing that it is.

Remember when that boyfriend who should have been grateful that you ever even gave him the time of day broke up with you for absolutely no reason? HE broke up with YOU? Consider him driven out by hornets. God is moving what needs to go out of your way. You're welcome.

But back to your current dream. Before you throw up your hands and quit, ask yourself if it's possible that you're asking for something that's bigger than what you are currently able to manage. Maybe God's answer is not "no"; maybe it's "Give Me a minute." The phrase "until you have increased enough" is a reference to the Israelites needing to grow enough to be able to take over the land He was clearing for them. God had been promising them this land for years. They would get it, but not now and not all at once. He explains that if He clears it too quickly, something even more problematic, wild animals, would move in before they could take over. Who's down for some pack of hyenas action? Me neither. So it's good news/bad news for the Hebrews: God's going to clear these people out for you, but it's going to be a long time before you actually get to move in. You're going to have to grow into it.

The fact that my efforts are under the authority of God's timing is a relief, really. It's protection. God isn't going to let me just go off half-cocked and take on more than I can handle, which I am incredibly prone to do. He tells me to keep trusting Him to clear the way little by little while I grow into it. Maybe God's waiting on me to increase enough. Maybe I need to grow in knowledge, in obedience, in being a person who doesn't sigh loudly and roll her eyes at the fact that Wal-Mart only has two lanes open on a Saturday morning in December. God has his reasons. Whatever they are, God is still here to bless me, not to harm me, to give me hope and a future, even when I'm not getting exactly what I want, exactly when I want it (see Jeremiah 29:11 paraphrase mine).

Don't be discouraged if you haven't seen a full answer to your prayers yet. Know that He hears you. The fact that the Most High God cares about our individual concerns and responds to us is almost unfathomable. But He does. Whether His response to us is spectacularly immediate or excruciatingly slow, it's all still miraculous.

So humble yourselves under the mighty power of God, and at the right time he will lift you up in honor. Give all your worries and cares to God, for he cares about you.

1 PETER 5:6–7

The Point

If God is delaying your plan, He's doing you a favor.

Journal Prompts

- What have you waited on for a long time?
- How do (did) you feel about waiting?
- What do you think about the idea that God might be doing you a favor with the delay?
- How does God's status as all-knowing and all-powerful affect your situation?

Let's Pray

Father God, you are El Elyon, the Most High God. Your greatness and sovereignty over all things is beyond my comprehension. Thank You that You know what You're doing at all times and You are always right. Thank You for looking out for me, even when I don't appreciate it. I'm sorry for all the smack I've talked in the process. Please help me to see things from Your perspective, to be patient and to increase in all the ways you want me to increase. Thank you for your promises and your timing.

To Play

"Better View" by Switch

The Judgement

For this is how God loved the world: He gave his one and only Son, so that everyone who believes in him will not perish but have eternal life. God sent his Son into the world not to judge the world, but to save the world through him.

JOHN 3:16-17

When my daughter was in the stroller stage, I spent copious hours walking the creekside trail behind our house with her, Sailor, and Tampa. We'd all start out strong, briskly following the curve of the canals, with Sailor and Eden almost running to keep up with the leisurely gait of myself and Tampa. By the time we passed the first bridge, the toddler would decide to ride in the stroller, content to leisurely feed herself goldfish and throw shoes rather than walk. Sailor, not to be outdone by Tampa, would strain to match her trot, though it meant a near sprint for him.

One day as I paused to retrieve a tennis shoe liberated by my free-toed toddler, an exhausted Sailor leaped into the bottom storage compartment of the stroller, panting like he might die. Hey, he knows a free ride when he sees one. From then on, when he would tire, he would simply stop and lie down in the road, mid-stride. We'd all pause, and he would jump the metal bar to his spot under the passenger seat. It was a perfectly charming solution. Such a clever boy.

Flash forward a decade. Our child had long outgrown a stroller, and, at 14, Sailor was no longer a dog who could jump over a bar into anything. He still loved a walk, but it was a slow one. Even on short trips, his legs tired, and he needed to be carried. My lower back is here to tell it. Thirteen pounds sounds light until you carry it for a mile or two.

For his fifteenth birthday, we got Sailor what all teenagers are hoping for, some wheels. Once again, he got to ride in the stroller, this time in the passenger seat. The day it arrived we all spent the day walking our city's riverside trails as fast as we wanted. You should have seen how happy Sailor was. It was a win for everyone. Sailor was no longer confined to slow, short walks. Sunflower, who was still a puppy, returned to her exuberant strut. And Sugarbell, who is easily overheated, could jump in the shady stroller when she needed a break. Sweet freedom! It was one of our very best days.

But then the judgment. When you walk a dog in a stroller, you get the side-eye. People have said some remarkably disparaging things, to my face, regarding our use of a dog stroller. They would see us pushing our happy, tongue-wagging dogs and jump to some interesting conclusions. They usually assumed one of two things:

1. that my husband and I were experiencing some sort of crazed empty-nest delirium and were trying to relive young parenthood via our dogs or

2. that our dogs were so spoiled that we didn't require them to walk.

Even though it was absolutely none of their business, I found myself explaining to complete strangers that we had a stroller because,

Hot-roddin'.

without it, one of our dogs was not physically able to enjoy walks, one of his favorite things.

Our family had a conundrum. We could either not let any of our dogs go for long walks, since Sailor couldn't participate, or we could leave him behind, watching from the front window, confused and heartbroken as we leashed up and departed with the younger dogs. No to both! People could side-eye me all day long. I wasn't resigning Sailor to a life of only watching from a window. I was giving Sailor his life back and a little shaming from strangers was not about to stop me.

On an exponentially greater scale, Christ looked at humanity and felt the same way. He resolved to rescue us from meaningless, hellbent lives, and no level of torture was about to stop Him. I have no reference for the level of sorrow and pain Christ endured for me. He and I are not rivals on the scale of sacrificial aptitude. My love for Sailor endured side-eye, while Jesus's love for me endured dying one of the most torturous means of execution in history.

The book of Luke recounts the crucifixion of Jesus: "When they came to a place called The Skull, they nailed him to the cross.... Jesus said, 'Father, forgive them, for they don't know what they're doing.' And the soldiers gambled for his clothes by throwing dice. The crowd watched and the leaders scoffed. 'He saved others,' they said, 'let him save himself if he is really God's Messiah, the Chosen One.' The soldiers mocked him, too, by offering him a drink of sour wine. They called out to him, 'If you are the King of the Jews, save yourself!' A sign was fastened above him with these words: 'This is the King of the Jews.' One of the criminals hanging beside him scoffed, 'So you're the Messiah, are you? Prove it by saving yourself—and us, too, while you're at it!'" (Luke 23:33–39).

Jesus endured both humiliation and physical torment to the point of death, because He knew that through His suffering we would be saved. Jesus could see the end of the story at the beginning. His singular mission was to redeem us, regardless of His personal pain. Even as he was being nailed to the cross, Jesus's concern was for his executioners rather than Himself, interceding on their behalf: "Father, forgive them, for they do not know what they are doing" (Luke 23:34 NIV). His unselfish love was not deterred by their cruelty. Jesus loved those people so much that it did not matter to Him what they had done or what they were currently doing. His heart was set on redeeming them.

The fact that Jesus chose to sacrifice Himself on our behalf is staggering. Though He had the power to escape, He allowed himself to be mocked, mercilessly beaten, then crucified. If you want to understand the full impact of this, research Roman flogging and crucifixion. It was brutal beyond modern comprehension. And Jesus chose to endure it so we could be made right with God.

Because of the joy awaiting him, he endured the cross, disregarding its shame.
HEBREWS 12:2

The Point

Jesus endured the pain of crucifixion to
save us because He loves us.

Journal Prompts

- When was a time that you had to endure embarrassment or physical pain to show kindness to another person (or pet)?
- Has anyone ever had to endure embarrassment or physical pain to show kindness to you?
- How do you feel when you consider that Jesus loved you enough to endure the cross?
- Read John, chapter 19, in the Bible and journal your thoughts.[24]

Let's Pray

Jesus, Your very name means "the Lord saves." You are the Messiah, our redeemer, our shepherd, healer, friend, savior, Almighty God. Thank You for saving us. Thank You for enduring the humiliation and pain of the cross. Thank You for Your strength and Your goodness. Thank You for offering me eternal life. Please forgive my sins and help me to grasp the magnitude of Your sacrifice for me.

To Play

"My Jesus" by Anne Wilson

---

24. If you don't have a Bible, download the free Bible app or go to www.bible.com. Click on "read the Bible now", then click on the top left "Genesis" for a drop-down menu, then click on "John", then on "Chapter 19".

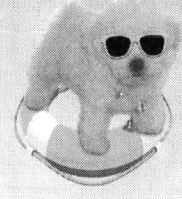

Made New

> I myself will tend my sheep and give them a place to lie down in peace, says the Sovereign LORD. I will search for my lost ones who strayed away, and I will bring them safely home again. I will bandage the injured and strengthen the weak.
>
> EZEKIEL 34:15-16

At the end of his life, Sailor developed neuropathy in his feet, which led him to walk on his toes rather than with a sure foot. Traversing our home's hardwoods took substantial effort. It was a tedious life for a boy who liked to follow his people from room to room all day. The other dogs would race to the kitchen the second they heard any hint of food prep. If I opened a cabinet door, Sunflower and Sugarbell immediately appeared at my feet. Meanwhile, Sailor would still be three rooms away, scrambling to arrive in time for treats. His struggle was unbearable to witness. So I started carrying him everywhere. If I was going to the kitchen, I'd just pick him up and take him with me. When we let him outside, we carried him down the front porch stairs, waited for him, then carried him back inside. We took a number of measures to make navigating our home easier, trying everything from ramps to rubberized walkways, which helped somewhat, but not enough.

Because of his mobility issues, Sailor frequently did not make it to the door when he needed to go out. Having been chastised many times for marking in the house (you'll recall my previous full rant), he knew that the bathroom was outside. He understood the expectation but was physically unable to meet it. When I would find another accident, he would lower his head in sheepish apology, expecting a reprimand. But at no point was I mad at him. His difficulty didn't agitate me; it grieved me. I didn't want to punish him for his weakness. I wanted to help him.

A few months after his fifteenth birthday, his back once again caused enough trouble to warrant the familiar treatment of crate-rest and medication. It was a miserable couple of weeks for him, but he seemed to be making his usual full recovery. By the end of treatment, he was cheerfully strolling the yard with me. He was back to his normal self. Then, without warning, he could barely walk. Then he refused to eat.

Anyone could see that Sailor had lived his full fifteen-year life expectancy and it was time to say goodbye. Anyone but me.

Sailor had made such dramatic and surprising recoveries in the past; I kept hoping that he would surprise me again. But we couldn't deny that it was time to consider letting him go. I wrestled with the thought, agonizing over the possibility that I might end his life prematurely. What if I made the choice to put him to sleep when he would have made a full recovery like the last time? I would lie beside his bed, coaxing him to take a little food from my hand, encouraged by his slightest interest, doing anything I could to rally him. If you could will someone to live, Sailor would be driving us crazy with his perennial licking of household surfaces right now.

When he stopped drinking water, I called the vet to make another appointment. The tech listened to my description of his behavior then matter of factly stated that I had an appointment at 5:30 p.m. to put him down. Just writing it, I could cry tears of shock again. Of course, it was obvious. But I was still in a hopeful state of denial. I had only meant to set an appointment to get some additional treatment that would return Sailor to his usual self. The tech assured me that if the vet had such a thing, she would share it at 5:30.

If I had it to do again, I would have totally ignored my to-do list that day, but the reality that those were my last hours with Sailor had not reached me. I spent the morning trying to pacify him while prepping for overnight Thanksgiving guests and dealing with HVAC people, since our furnace chose that week to die too. It was a heck of a morning.[25]

Fortunately, by noon I got my priorities straight and spent the rest of the day holding Sailor and letting him say goodbye to his favorite things, even though I didn't really believe it would be goodbye (the mind is a mystery). I took him to all of his favorite places to hide and/or pee on. Then we sat on the backyard swing and talked about feral cats and bike rides. I guess somewhere during the day the truth became undeniable, even to me, because I took him for what I knew would be the last ride in his new stroller. I stopped, sat on the curb, looked him in his tired eyes, and told him that he was just exactly the little dog I had always hoped for and how much I loved him. And then I told him it was okay to go.

And now I have something in my eye. Hang on.

---

25. A word about friendship: my friend Amy saw a social media post I had made that morning and just showed up at my house to sit on the kitchen floor with me and tell Sailor goodbye. She also found a photo of him in a social media album, then pirated it, printed it, lettered his name on it (cause she's crafty like that), then framed it. This is one of the most thoughtful things anyone has ever done for me. A friend who stops their day to show up in your sorrow is a rare and beautiful thing.

By the time Jeff and I carried him into the vet's office, she told me to just hold him; he was almost gone. Since Sailor never liked the vet's office (what dog does?), but loved car rides, we got back in the car where I rubbed his downy ears and talked softly to him as he passed.

God is so kind. It was such a gift to me that I did not have to put Sailor down that day and then worry that I had made the wrong decision. My own regret is that I didn't let him go before his last miserable day.

I laid Sailor, still wrapped in his blanket, on the table before our veterinarian. As she uncovered him, I gasped. It was as if he had transformed into his younger self in the time it took for me to walk from the car to her exam room. He looked so much like he had as a baby that it brought fresh tears to my eyes. Even the vet said something about how, for a fifteen-year-old dog, he still looked like a puppy.

Because of his disc issues, Sailor had walked with weak back legs and a rounded back for some time. But when he passed, his body unclenched and straightened. He looked like he might spring up and zoom around the office. It really was as if he was a puppy again. While I was devastated to lose my sweet buddy, it was a blessing to see so clearly that his struggles and the pain were over.

Sailor's physical transformation is a picture of the renewal that we as believers will experience when we pass from this life into eternal life. The contrast between the suffering we acquire through earthly hardship and the new life that Jesus promises is stark. In the book of Revelation, God's Word assures us that our eternal future is one without sorrow or pain or death (see Revelation 21:4).

This life is only temporary. It's a sad fact of life that every one of us will die. But death is not the end. God has made arrangements for us to pass from this life into a better one. Jesus died and rose again so that anyone who believes in Him will have eternal life (see John 3:16). And that is extremely good news!

As for my sweet Sailor, the Bible doesn't say for certain what happens to pets when they die, but I like to imagine him in heaven, running figure-eights through a field, pain free, ears flapping. Maybe with Tampa. I don't know. But I hope that when I get there, he'll be the first to greet me.

He will wipe every tear from their eyes, and there will be no more death or sorrow or crying or pain. All these things are gone forever. And the one sitting on the throne said, "Look, I am making everything new!"

REVELATION 21:4-5

The Point

Physical death is not the end,
but the beginning of a whole new life.

Journal Prompts

- Have you had the experience of losing someone (person or pet) you loved to physical death?
- Was it comforting to know that their suffering had ended?
- When you read the promise of Revelation 21:4–5, how do you think of death?
- What do you imagine it's like in heaven?

Let's Pray

Lord, You are El-Olam, the eternal, never-ending creator of the universe. You are beyond my comprehension, as eternity is beyond comprehension. Thank You for salvation through Jesus so we can be with You in eternity. Thank You that there will be no death or crying or sorrow. Thank You that You do make everything new.

To Play

"I Can Only Imagine" by Mercy Me

Sailor Napoleon Catfish Johnson
September 3, 2004 – November 25, 2019

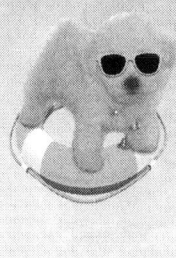

Q & A

On the following pages, you'll find explanations for some things I mention in the chapters that might not be familiar. I hope it answers the questions you might have.

How can I know God?

First, know that God is holy. He has no flaws and is perfect in His goodness. Second, know that people are sinners. We make mistakes. Therefore, we are separated from God. People are like muddy boots, and God is like your favorite plush white rug. Those boots are not getting anywhere near that rug—right? It's an oversimplification, but you get the idea. Since God is holy (white rug) and people are sinners (muddy boots), we are separated. To come to God we need something to clean us up and bridge the separation.

John 3:16 is probably the most well-known verse in the Bible. It tells us that "God so loved the world that he gave his one and only Son [Jesus], that whoever believes in him shall not perish but have eternal life" (NIV).

Jesus died on the cross and rose again to pay for all of our sins. He was the final sacrifice. Through Him, we can have a relationship with

God and receive eternal life. Jesus removes our sin (mud). He bridges the chasm between us and God. "I am the way, and the truth, and the life. No one comes to the Father except through me" (John 14:6 ESV).

So how do you accept Jesus and become a child of God? Great question. God's Word promises that "If you openly declare that Jesus is Lord and believe in your heart that God raised him from the dead, you will be saved. For it is by believing in your heart that you are made right with God, and it is by openly declaring your faith that you are saved" (Romans 10:9–10). Isn't that shockingly simple?

If you would like to invite Jesus into your life, you can pray something like this: "Jesus, I believe You are the son of God and that You died for me and rose again. Please forgive me for my sins and come into my life. Be my Lord and Savior." Simple as it is, if you sincerely pray this prayer, it will be the beginning of a whole new life for you. "This means that anyone who belongs to Christ has become a new person. The old life is gone; a new life has begun!" (2 Corinthians 5:17).

When you accept Christ as Savior, you are given the Holy Spirit. The Bible says that God "has identified us as his own by placing the Holy Spirit in our hearts as the first installment that guarantees everything He promised us" (2 Corinthians 1:21–22). God's own Spirit now lives within you to guide, encourage, and comfort you. The Holy Spirit is always with you as a friend and helper.

Now "openly declare your faith" by telling someone about your decision. And get ready! I don't know what God's gonna do in your life, but I know it's gonna be GOOD!

And here's one last song because it's so very fitting: "New Day" by Danny Gokey.

So what next?

- Visit Christian churches near you. It's important to be in a community with other believers and to have a place where you can learn more about God. Try www.arcchurches.com/find-a-church if you don't know where to start. Church of the Highlands in Birmingham, Alabama, changed my life. They're a megachurch now, but I was there when they first started and the experience changed everything I thought about church and church people. As they would say, it went "from a have-to to a get-to." Keep searching until you find a place that fits you, then get involved as a volunteer and join a small group. That's how you'll find community. You need friends who share your faith.

* Jesus modeled being baptized in water. It symbolizes going from our old life to new life. When you find a church you like, ask them about baptism.

* To grow in your new relationship with God, spend time reading the Bible and talking with Him. I highly recommend finding devotionals that you can study every day. Any retail store that sells books will have a selection in the Christian living section. If you sincerely pursue learning about God and spending time with Him, you'll be shocked by the amazing, miraculous things that will happen in your life!

I've created a PDF listing some of my favorite apps, podcasts and other resources for you. It's free at pages.pup-epiphanies.com/resources

What if I don't know how to pray?

The disciples asked Jesus how to pray, so He modeled a prayer, known as the "Lord's Prayer," in Matthew 6:9–13. That's our best example and guide for how to approach God in prayer, but don't be intimidated. Prayer is very simple. It doesn't have to be fancy. Just talk to

God as you would talk to a friend about whatever's on your mind. You can use any of the prayers at the end of chapters as guides, then add your own thoughts and questions. I'll break the basic components of prayer down to help you get started.

1. "You're awesome." What do you find amazing about God? Tell Him. That's worship. "Exalt the LORD our God! Bow low before his feet, for he is holy!" (Psalm 99:5).

2. "Thank you." Thank God for the things in your life that you're grateful for. All good things come from Him. "Enter his courts with thanksgiving, go into his courts with praise. Give thanks to Him and praise His name" (Psalm 100:4).

3. "I'm sorry." We all make mistakes. Ask for forgiveness for your sins and forgive others (though it may take time to *feel* like you've forgiven them, you can still *agree* to forgive them with God's help). "But if we confess our sins to him, he is faithful and just to forgive us our sins and to cleanse us from all wickedness" (1 John 1:9). God always forgives us when we ask.

4. "Please help." He has promised to hear us when we pray and to help in times of trouble. What are you concerned about? What is your hope? Talk to Him about it. "Give all your worries and cares to God, for He cares about you" (1 Peter 5:7).

What if I don't have a Bible?

- Check out the free Bible app (the one developed by Life.Church), also referred to as "YouVersion." There are so many resources on this app including many translations of the Bible, devotionals, and video teachings.

- Any church will likely have a hard copy Bible they'll give you for free, if you just ask.
- You can also buy affordable Bibles online or in stores. I highly recommend getting one that is considered a study Bible, because it will have footnotes to help you understand what you're reading.

How do I choose a Bible translation?

Most of the verses I quote in this book are from the New Living Translation (NLT), because it uses modern, easy-to-understand language. The New International Version (NIV), the New American Standard Bible (NASB), and the English Standard Version (ESV) are also excellent choices. They more precisely translate word for word from the original languages, but the style is less conversational than the NLT.

What do you mean by "worship"?

The word "worship" can be used in many different contexts to have different meanings (for instance, a worship service or a worship center). What I'm talking about is intentionally thinking about the wonderful attributes of God. Anything that helps you meditate on God in a grateful manner is worship. You could be outside listening to the wind blow. Just concentrate on God and tell Him all the things you appreciate about Him.

Listening to Christian worship music is a great way to focus your attention and admiration on God. I've included some worship songs by popular artists as recommendations within the chapters (for instance, "The Goodness of God" by Bethel), but there are many more.

A word about mental health

If you are struggling with an emotional crisis, addiction, intrusive thoughts, self-harm, or suicidal thoughts, I encourage you to seek assistance from trained counselors in addition to taking spiritual steps. There are wonderful Christian mental health counselors who can help you walk through recovery from trauma while helping you experience the transforming power of God in your life.

- Find free counseling and referrals at focusonthefamily.com/counseling.

- Many churches can also refer you to local Christian counselors.

- If you are struggling with suicidal thoughts, please call the National Suicide Prevention Lifeline at 1-800-273-8255 or text "TALK" to 741-741.

I am not a mental health counselor or medical professional. Please seek treatment from a physician or a certified mental health counselor if you are struggling with any mental health issues, intrusive thoughts of self-harm, or suicidal thoughts.

*Don't be afraid, for I am with you.
Don't be discouraged, for I am your God.
I will strengthen you and help you.
I will hold you up with my victorious right hand.*

ISAIAH 41:10

Acknowledgements

If you're reading this, thank you for helping me acknowledge the people who helped me get Pup-epiphanies out of my head and into the world.

You'd think that publishing a short book is pretty simple. It is not. I didn't know what I didn't know. (If you'd ever like to have a long and boring conversation about ISBN numbers hit me up.) Let's just say there were many people who contributed to this little book. And I'm so very grateful!

Thank you to my wildly supportive husband, Jeff. First, I wouldn't have puppies if you hadn't adopted them with me, so thanks for being game. Second, I'm blown away by how genuinely you support (endure) my creative ventures. You have listened to me read something "one more time" more times than I can count. And you let me to tell the truth even when it isn't our best side. There's no one I'd rather roll under the bus with than you.

And to the sweetest blessing of my life, Eden, thank you for allowing me to include some of your story here. As much as I loved Sailor, it's nothing compared to how much I love you, LD. I'm inspired by your genuine desire to know the Lord and help others know Him too. Your contributions have made this book (and my life) infinitely better.

Thank you to CJ and Shelley Hitz of Christian Book Academy. This book would still be scraps of paper in a drawer somewhere if not for your practical and spiritual mentorship.

Getting a book to print is a process, but even if I get the technical stuff wrong, it's not really going to matter in the grand scheme of things. However, if I get the Biblical stuff wrong, it does matter. Thank God I have some amazingly kind, generous, and studied women in my life. I am so very grateful to you Kelli, Linda, Harriett, Angela, Karen, and Shari for being my mentors, leaders, friends, and inspirations. Your wise and insightful notes made *Pup-epiphanies* exponentially better. Thank you for your lavish generosity of thought and time and friendship.

Thank you, Lee, for your trusted leadership, encouragement and generous support.

Thank you to Linda, Alice and Chrissy for sharing your time, insight and encouragement.

To the girls in my FUSE group: Your honest questions have helped shape this book. You're the head and not the tail!

Thank you, Rita, for being a wonderful neighbor and for feeding all of God's creatures.

Thank you, Amy, for being a friend of kindness and crafts.

Thanks to my mom, Glenda, for always listening with a "that's good, real good," as a mom should. I appreciate your encouragement. Thanks to my dad, Ron, for bringing home puppies, even if you eventually have to shoot over their head to make them shut up. (And for letting me tell everybody about it.) And thank you both for raising me in a home where God was welcome.

Thank you, Miata, my favorite car I ever owned. As a short person, it was a revelation to be able to reach something I dropped in the passenger floorboard without having to pull over.

Thank you, UPS, for your courteous drivers. It's no wonder "dogs of UPS" is a thing.

Acknowledgements

Thank you, Mr. McConaughey, for setting a standard of cool to which we can all aspire.

Thanks to Swiffer for not being a broom. I knew my life had taken a serious turn when I found myself talking about how much I loved my Swiffer at a party.

Thanks to The Bible Recap and Bible Project for the utterly amazing learning tools.

And thanks to Tampa, Sailor, Sugarbell, Sunflower, and Clover for giving me so many stories. And for being mostly house-trained.

And thank YOU for reading the book *and* the acknowledgments. I am fully aware that reading this list is akin to watching the seventeen-person creative team of a short film you never even heard of crowd the stage at the Oscars to thank their wives and children and middle school teachers, each struggling to the mic as the music rises. (Speaking of, thank you to my eighth grade English teacher, Ms. Marler, for teaching me to love a good story— you could tell one. And also for teaching me how to, more or less, know where to put commas.)

And mostly, thank you, LORD, for giving me the undeserved privilege of writing this book about You and me and Sailor. I hope you like it.

Author Bio

Leslie Vicary is a wife, mom, and dog mom. When she's not navigating after-school car lines like a boss, she prides herself on being the most middle-aged, suburbanite on any dance floor, though she has grudgingly promised her husband to never again "stir the pot" (in public; it's still very much in play at the house). Leslie is a product of the American South, boasting an enviable lineage of cotton pickers, coalminers, and Mary Kay ladies. She graduated from the University of Alabama with a degree in communication and a minor in theatre, which has proven to be predictably useless. Roll Tide. Leslie lives with her husband Jeff, her daughter Eden, and Sugarbell, Sunflower, and Clover near Greenville, South Carolina, where they attend NewSpring Church—not the dogs, just the people. This is her first book, but it won't be her last because it's a series.

instagram.com/leslievicary

facebook.com/leslievicary.writer

Thank You For Reading My Book!

If you enjoyed *God Loves You as Much as You Love Your Dog*, I'd really appreciate a review. I love hearing what you have to say and more reviews help more people find this book.

Please take two minutes to leave a review now.

Scan here to leave a review:

Thank you,
Leslie V.

WANT MORE?

Sign up for the
Pup-epiphanies Newsletter!

A few times a month I send out new writing about whatever's amusing and inspiring me. Plus you'll get special offers and updates on new releases in the Pup-epiphanies book series.

SIGN UP NOW!
pages.pup-epiphanies.com/newsletter

Unsubscribe whenever you want.

Made in the USA
Middletown, DE
24 December 2022

17373702R00084